Chasing

Love

CHASING

LOVE

Morod K. Zayed

Let the Light In

In loving memory of Jeff Coleman

I don't know if I would have made it through the darkest days of my life without you. You were more than a manager and mentor, you were like a father to me and I miss you every day.

Contents

Based on a true story...

CHAPTER 1

Lunch with John

The tears fell slowly and in rhythm with the leaky faucet as I gazed upon the reflection staring back at me. The cracked mirror above the bathroom sink said so much without uttering a word. Standing there, I wondered how this could have happened to me.

January, 1995. The bell rang and all across Canton High School, classrooms emptied as students stormed the hallways. Some headed to their next class, but for others like me, it was the beginning of lunch period. As a scrawny sophomore, I took every opportunity to lighten the weight of my backpack so I made a brief stop at my locker before continuing on to the cafeteria. By the time I arrived, the cafeteria had become heavily crowded with hundreds of students gathered in groups of all sizes. I scanned the room in search of the two familiar faces I had spent the previous semester eating lunch with, but they were nowhere to be found. As the minutes passed and the remaining empty seats quickly filled up, my inability to secure a place to sit created a sense of panic within me. I paced up and down the rows of lunch tables, as my anxiety and desperation escalated. In that moment, I would have settled for *any* student willing to sit with me. Just one student, that's all I was looking for. The former version of myself might have considered eating alone but he no longer existed. What remained was a young teenager so tightly imprisoned by fear that just about everything seemed more challenging than it needed to be, especially meeting new people. I had become an overly insecure 15-year-old, who was desperate to avoid further rejection at all cost—no doubt a byproduct from the wounds I carried inside me that had never healed. Some of these wounds dated back to my childhood while others were more recent, inflicted upon me a year earlier as a high school freshman.

From the onset, high school had been difficult for me. As a short and skinny freshman, I made for an easy target for a couple of upperclassmen bullies who plucked me out from the crowd. Adding fuel to their hatred of underclassmen was my Middle Eastern background, which resulted in having to endure racial slurs, being called everything from an *A-Rab* to a *camel jockey*. Although I was never physically attacked, these bullies kept me in a continuous state of fear with frequent reminders that, at any time, they had the ability to beat me up. Knowing this could happen, I began to alter my daily routine at school, from which hallways I walked down to where I sat on the bus. But my efforts were unsuccessful as they continued their verbal onslaught for months. The experience certainly took its toll on me but paled in comparison to the betrayal I suffered at the hands of my closest friends—the neighborhood boys I had grown up with.

Friends No More

Raised in a home with only sisters, these boys were the brothers I never had. In addition to the years of playing every sport imaginable, we hung out at local stores buying candy and cherry flavored slushes, and spent countless summer days trading baseball cards, playing videos games and hanging out on our parents' front porches. But when I needed them most, to help fend off the bullies, my supposed "friends" were nowhere to be found. Not only did none of them defend me, a couple even decided to join in on the bullying. The worst betrayal happened on the school bus, where one friend in particular would spit on me and painfully flick my ears on a constant basis. It was a daily battle to hold in tears over the shame and embarrassment I felt for not being able to defend myself. Things had escalated to a point where I was forced to sit alone at the front of the bus near the driver for protection. The bullying continued until I finally reported it to a school counselor. To her credit, she was able to stop the harassment; but by then, the damage was done.

This experience had essentially reinforced a poor view I already had about myself – *I wasn't good enough to be cared for nor was I worthy enough to be loved.* It was a seed that was planted during my formative years in a house where love had to be earned and perfection was all but required. My parents were disciplinarians, masters at imposing tough love on my sisters and me. Their love was conditional, needing to be earned every step of the way. If I wasn't good enough for my own parents to love me unconditionally, I had no business thinking I'd fare any better with the neighborhood kids.

After the experience with the bullies and my friends, I became withdrawn, finding it difficult to open up—let alone trust anyone. I spent the remaining months of freshman year with my head down and mouth shut. I focused on my grades and did my best to avoid friendships at all cost. Isolation was the only place I knew. The place I felt comfortable. It was my safe haven.

By the time sophomore year began, my self-imposed exile from the previous school year had left me without a single friend. The only interruption from solitude occurred during lunch after I had inadvertently found myself eating with two random students. The three of us were quiet, anti-social kids using each other's company to avoid the embarrassment of having to eat alone. Although we sat together for much of the first semester, we seldom engaged in conversation outside of infrequent pleasantries. We ate quickly, working hard to avoid being the last one left at the lunch table each day. The arrangement wasn't great but it served its purpose. That is until the start of the second semester arrived and with it a change to my lunch period. This change ruined the routine and those two students were nowhere to be found. And I was now utterly alone.

And there you have it. That is how I found myself pacing around the cafeteria that first day of the second semester of my sophomore year, desperate to find a place to eat lunch. And when I realized I was the only student still looking for a place to sit, I rushed toward the nearest exit sign. Once out in the hallway, I eventually calmed down and sought a better outcome by visiting the cafeteria across campus at the other high school.

Hunger Pains

My high school was one of two schools that shared a large, college-like campus, home to over 5,000 students. The setup was unique and by most accounts, well-liked by students. The sheer size of the two schools provided an increased opportunity to meet people, and yet somehow I still found myself alone. By the time I made my way across campus, lunch was now more than halfway through and most students were just about finishing up their meals. Standing at the entrance of the cafeteria, I stood there frozen, contemplating my next steps. Should I brave it out, enter the cafeteria, sit down, and make good on the short time left for lunch, or should I make a U-turn down the hallway? I silenced all the background noise coming from the cafeteria and weighed my options. I began to imagine sitting alone, and the fear of being laughed out of the cafeteria completely overwhelmed me. I did what any other skinny, frail, friendless, broken, rejected, insecure kid would do: I threw my lunch in the garbage and walked out disheartened. With an empty and growling stomach, I found it difficult to concentrate during the remaining classes that day. Hunger was an issue, but it took a backseat to the realization that I was likely to face this same scenario the next day…and perhaps many more days to come.

Tuesday, day two of the semester. The bell rang for lunch but this time I decided to cross campus instead, hoping to have more luck visiting the other school's cafeteria first. I walked at a brisk pace, but by the time I arrived, students were already gathered together with their friends and all the tables were full. I stood there at the entrance and similar to the events that played out the prior day, I was paralyzed by fear. The voices in my head were quick to remind me that I was a loser with no friends and that everyone was staring at me because I was still standing with no place to eat lunch. Terrified of drawing unwanted attention, I concluded that I had no business being there in the first place and for a second consecutive day, I threw my lunch in the garbage and walked out of the cafeteria with my head hanging low.

Wednesday came and, having been so discouraged by how things had played out the first two days, I didn't bother going to either cafeteria. Instead, I roamed around like a lost puppy, walking up and down the hallways as well as back and forth between both schools until lunch was over.

Day four mirrored the previous day, as I made no attempt to enter either cafeteria. But while I was aimlessly wandering around, I happened to walk past an area in the school called The Pit. It was the "cool" spot where athletes, cheerleaders and the popular students hung out, serving as their own private mingling area between classes and during lunch. The students hanging out there were all cut from the same cloth—good looking, wearing expensive and trendy clothes, laughing without a care in the world. They were the *masters* of the high school universe and I harbored a deep sense of jealousy toward them. These students appeared to have it easy and, in comparison to what I was dealing with, their world looked perfect. As I walked away, I thought about all I would have given up to be part of their world—even if it included selling my soul to the devil.

Friday came, day five of the semester, and the misery continued as I stared down another uncertain lunch period. Once again I found myself near the Pit, taking in the view of the popular kids and the good life. I looked on in envy, wondering if someone would discern the hurting soul standing in front of them. Maybe if I got noticed, one of these cool kids would invite me into their exclusive group. But that's not how things work in high school. You're either popular or you're not. *And I was not.* I stood there completely ignored by everyone as if I were invisible; the reality being that I was.

The school day ended the same as it had the previous four days, with me going hungry. After I got off the bus, I cried while walking the final two blocks home, unsure of how I was going to survive an entire semester without any friends and never eating at school. I needed help but I was too embarrassed to share my struggles with my sisters or my parents out of fear they would be ashamed of me. What I was desperate for was compassion, support, and love, but those weren't things I had much experience with at home. Opening up to family was an invitation for more ridicule so I decided to keep it all bottled up inside. That night, I buried myself deep under the covers of my bed and I cried my heart out. Using my pillow to muffle the sounds of my hurt, I sobbed until the tears ran dry.

Prior to that night, I had never prayed before. But finding my face in a puddle of tears, I was desperate and out of options so I crawled out of my bed and onto my knees. Even though I was raised in a Christian household, I knew little about praying and even less about God. My parents rarely talked about God, and church attendance was usually limited to Easter, Christmas, weddings, and funerals. From my perspective, believing in God was nothing more than a family tradition. I don't even recall them mentioning God at all except, of course, during Easter when I'd see my parents watching old Jesus movies on TV. Those movies did nothing except confuse me, especially the part where Jesus was God but he was also human. That made absolutely no sense whatsoever. And what was the cross thing all about? Jesus was crucified and, because of it, I go to heaven when I die? All of it seemed way too perplexing and, dare I say...fictitious.

So, with no foundation in faith, I struggled in those first few moments as I fumbled around trying to find the right words to say. Was there a specific formula I needed to follow, certain steps I needed to take in order for God to listen to me? Uneducated in the ways of prayer, I simply looked up toward the ceiling and I asked - or rather - begged God to help me:

"Please, please, please make me popular so that I have friends, and so I don't have to eat my lunch alone. Make me popular like the kids who hang out at the Pit. I promise if you answer this prayer I'll never ask for another thing for the rest of my life."

My words were neither eloquent nor articulate but they were the best I had to offer. My request seemed reasonable, certainly not too difficult for a God who was supposedly the creator of the universe. I sat there for several minutes in silence waiting, staring at the ceiling, desperately hoping for something. I don't know what I expected to happen that night, but it didn't matter. God was silent and eventually my patience and energy wore out. I slipped back into bed and under the covers. I couldn't help but think that desperation will lead you down just about any road, even one as foolish as praying to God.

Let's Try This Again

When Monday arrived, I knew I was on my own. God was nowhere to be found and I was left to fend for myself. I needed to find a solution for my lunch troubles, and avoiding the cafeteria the way I had done the previous week wasn't it. So when the lunch bell rang, I ran toward the cafeteria, palms sweating and feet moving at full speed. I stood at the entrance doors this time determined to find a table to sit at regardless if I ate alone. But right on cue, fear took hold of me and my feet refused to move, as if they had been nailed to the floor. The time for mulling over my decision to not enter the cafeteria was interrupted as the crowds of students began pushing through the entrance, forcing me to the side. Completely deflated, I sat down on a bench nearby and watched as hundreds of students piled into the cafeteria.

Feeling the heaviness of tears hanging on my eyelids, I sunk my head deep into my puffy, black winter coat trying to conceal my identity. After what felt like an eternity, I composed myself enough to look beyond the inside of my coat. That's when the hallway leading away from the cafeteria and toward the far end of the building caught my attention. I'm not sure why this particular hallway appealed to me, but it did, and so I headed toward it. When the path ended, I was forced into the only remaining direction—up the staircase and toward the second floor. I peered down a long narrow hallway lined with lockers, and after taking a handful of steps forward I stopped, leaned up against the lockers, and allowed my body to slide down until I hit the floor. Unable to hold in the emotions any longer, I sat there on the floor with my head pressed against the lockers, feeling like a complete failure, tears uncontrollably pouring down my cheeks. Why did high school have to be so hard? Why was I so afraid of getting close to people? What was wrong with me?

After a few minutes with only the sounds of sniffling breaking the silence, I realized that not a single person had entered the hallway the entire time I had been sitting there. Instinctively, I unzipped my book bag, pulled out my lunch, and began eating right there on the floor. It wasn't ideal, but it was necessary. And after an entire week of not eating lunch at school, a peanut butter and jelly sandwich had never tasted so good. The relief was short-lived as two boys entered the hallway and headed straight toward me. I assumed I had been caught so I tried to hide the evidence by quickly shoving what remained of my lunch into my backpack. I braced myself for ridicule, but instead I was completely ignored and these two boys walked past me as if they hadn't even noticed me.

The next day, I found my way back to that same second-floor hallway and just like the previous day, it was completely empty. I sat down on the floor and leaned back against the lockers, this time a little further down the hallway. But just as I began to unzip my backpack, I heard footsteps thumping the staircase and suddenly a few boys were headed in my direction. I couldn't tell if they were the same students from the previous day, and I didn't want to stick around to find out. I got up off the floor and hurried in the opposite direction of the students and the stairs. And that's when I noticed the boy's bathroom between the rows of lockers. Not knowing what else to do, I escaped inside.

Breathing heavily, as though my chest was about to explode, I stood there in the middle of this small bathroom, unsure of what to do next. I peered at my reflection in the cracked mirror, took a few steps toward it, and then dropped my backpack on the edge of the sink. I could see tears beginning to well up in my eyes. I felt so alone, so afraid, so...ashamed. The silence in the bathroom was abruptly broken by the sound of my stomach growling and, without realizing what I was doing, I unzipped my backpack and used it as a plate and began eating right there in the bathroom. Terrified that someone might walk in, I quickly scarfed down my lunch while the reflection of a scared, and teary-eyed boy stared back at me.

The next day I was back in that same second-floor bathroom. And once again, I dropped my backpack on the sink, unzipped it, took out each food item one at a time and ate. I repeated this routine day after day, week after week and month after month, turning that secluded second-floor bathroom at the far end of the school into my private lunch room. I rarely had visitors; but when I did, I would throw whatever food I was eating into my backpack and begin finger-combing my hair to act as if I was just in there grooming myself. From the echoes of voices in the hallways to the sound of the creaking door announcing someone's presence, I perfected the ability to identify each and every noise I heard in the bathroom in order to avoid getting caught. And so things went on this way for the rest of the semester. Each day I ended up in that bathroom, standing at the sink, looking into the cracked mirror, and watching myself eat lunch. And each day I wondered why life had ended up this way and what I had done so wrong to deserve a punishment so severe. The initial relief of being able to eat lunch had long faded and what remained was anger as I began passionately hating the reflection staring back at me.

I had become a prisoner, with only my tears to keep me company in that bathroom—my tears and that mirror, *that damn mirror* that relentlessly taunted me with daily reminders that I was all alone. And as the days passed, the mirror continued its barrage of insults about how ugly I was, how short I was, how skinny I was, how dumb I was…how unlovable I was. The attacks didn't stop there. Eventually, the mirror began to spew its most brutal words – that nobody would ever care about me and that I was better off dead. And with each day and each attack, my cries to God got louder and more desperate. I begged him for reprieve from the endless torment coming from the mirror. I pleaded for God to show mercy, for him to fill the emptiness that had become a part of me. But the only thing God did was ignore me. He left me stranded in that dirty, smelly, disgusting bathroom, indifferent to my cries for help. 5,000 students and there I was, all alone, standing in front of that cracked mirror eating my lunch with John.

CHAPTER 2

Friends with Benefits

The last bell finally rang, ending what had been a horrific sophomore year. I had somehow survived a semester of eating lunch in the bathroom and without anyone knowing the hell I had been through. The experience had taken its toll on me, both mentally and emotionally, but I was determined to keep my dirty secret locked away. I wanted nothing more than to run far away from school and that bathroom, and never look back. With the school year now over, I shifted my attention to working. It was all I could do to erase the stench of shame I was carrying.

I returned to my job as a caddie at Meadowbrook, a private country club, for the start of my second summer of work. I was hired the previous year, and at the time, I knew absolutely nothing about golf or what a caddie did, but when my mom suggested a summer job, I jumped at the opportunity. Having spent the first half of my freshman year, being bullied and the second half with no friends, a job had a lot more appeal than spending a lonely summer hiding in my bedroom. So, in the spring of my freshman year I attended caddie training and officially became a Beginner, or *B Caddie*, within a couple of weeks. Sporting a buzz cut and a stern face, a slightly taller and heavier than average man walked in and laid out his rules and expectations. His name was Jeff and he was the manager that oversaw everything related to golf. His long list of rules included having to be clean-shaven every day, requiring our shirts to be tucked in at all times, and always addressing the members with "Yes, sir", "No, sir", "Yes, ma'am", or "No, ma'am". And then of course there was my *favorite* rule, the one I found to be the most ridiculous of all – arriving to work on time was considered being late by his standards. He came off like a dictator and, needless to say, I didn't care much for Jeff right from the start.

Among other things, Jeff's responsibilities included assigning caddies to members playing golf. His knowledge of which members tipped well influenced a caddie's assignment each day. Experienced caddies and those who were well-liked caddied for the highest tipping members, while unknown B caddies like myself were typically assigned to members who tipped lower on the recommended pay scale. In addition to being paid less, B caddies often logged many hours of unpaid time waiting around for Jeff to assign them a member to caddie for. In order to bypass the waiting, caddies could sign up to work two rounds of golf each day, and by doing so, would be assigned to a member early in the morning so they would be finished in time to caddie for another member in the afternoon. However, the hot and humid Michigan summer temperatures and what was equivalent to walking roughly five miles with a heavy golf bag on your shoulders detoured most caddies from afternoon work.

Although I was scrawny, I was determined to impress Jeff by doing what most caddies wouldn't do, so I began signing up to work two rounds each day. The work was exhausting, but I did it, and I did it well. About six weeks into the job, Jeff called me into his office one afternoon. I had just finished up for the day and was waiting for my mom to pick me up when he tapped on the glass from inside his office and motioned for me to come in. Fearing the worst, I entered assuming I was in trouble; instead, I was greeted with a short speech on how well I was doing. Jeff commended my work ethic and respectful demeanor, and also mentioned that several members had provided him with positive feedback as well. He shook my hand then handed me a new badge, one that read: *A Caddie*. I had just been promoted! The feeling of that new badge in my hand was like nothing I had ever felt. It validated my hard work but more importantly, it was the first time in my life I felt worthy, like I was really good at something. Working hard got me noticed and appreciated, two things I was desperate for, and it lit a fire inside me.

Hole in One

Jeff's recognition and continued encouragement motivated me to work even harder than I had been working and that first summer I continued to caddie as much as I could. I'd arrive early and work all day, sometimes spending ten or twelve hours a day at the golf course. As I continued putting in the long hours, Jeff continued to reward me. Right before the year's biggest tournament in August, the Men's Invitational, Jeff promoted me again, this time to *Captain Caddie*. When the golf season was over, I had caddied over 100 rounds of golf, which was the third highest total of all the caddies that year. At the year-end banquet that was held to honor us caddies, I won a TV! Not too bad for a 15-year-old working his first job.

What a summer it had been! Not only had I made good money but I had also been recognized for my hard work. It was the first time I can recall ever feeling like I mattered in this world. I was a completely different person at work and that feeling of having value was something I desperately needed. And Jeff, the boss who I thought was somewhat of a jerk when I first met him, turned out to be a really great guy after all. He was still a tough boss but I soon began to understand that he managed from a place of love, his way to instill work ethic and discipline into us teenage boys. Jeff made me feel special and I completely bought into everything he was teaching. I had learned a lot from him that first year, and by the year's end, I began to view Jeff less like my boss and more like a loving and caring father.

And to think that that entire first summer almost never happened because I had quit after my first day of work. Right after getting the job, I had signed up to caddie for the first tournament of the year, the Men's Get Acquainted. That first day was miserable. Not only did I arrive late but it rained throughout the entire tournament. With no jacket and no sweater, I spent five hours freezing on that cold and windy Saturday in May. When my mom picked me up and we were heading home, I could tell she was eager to hear details.

"Tell me, tell me...how did your first day go?"

"It sucked, Mom. I thought they said it wasn't going to rain today. I'm freezing and I'm soaking wet! I was there all day long and made fourteen bucks! A lousy fourteen bucks! And the member I caddied for yelled at me for making a mistake. This job sucks! I'm never going back."

"I'm sorry, honey. It's okay, though. I don't think you should give up yet. It was just the first day and it will get better. Tomorrow will be better."

When we arrived home, I didn't even make it to my bedroom. I was so worn out that I fell asleep on the family room carpet. I woke up several hours later, sore and aching from head to toe, vowing to never caddie again. My mom, however, had something different in mind. The next morning, she was standing by my bed gently nudging me awake at 6 a.m.

"Time to go to work."

I rolled over with my eyes still mostly closed. "Don't you remember what I said yesterday? I hate that job. I'm never going back."

"Sweetie, you need to give it another chance. It was your first day. It will get better with more experience."

Realizing she wasn't going to leave my room, I got up and dressed for work. Thirty minutes later, I was begrudgingly exiting my mom's car, not excited in the least bit to be back at work for another day of misery. But that second day went a lot differently than the first had. The sun was out, the temperature was much warmer, and the member I caddied for was a lot nicer. I even made $16 for that round, $2 more than I had the previous day.

Mom was right; things did get better, a lot better. And in addition to helping me get the job and not allowing me to quit when I wanted to, she made a tremendous sacrifice of her time by essentially becoming my personal chauffeur. The commute to work was twenty minutes each way on a good day, and I wasn't old enough to drive which meant she had to drive me to and from work every day. This was long before cell phones were a common fixture in everyday society, so my mom was essentially a prisoner in her own house, waiting around all day until I called her ready to be picked up. She did this regularly as I was working almost every day. This selfless act was the only reason I was able to work as much as I did. I never appreciated the sacrifice my mom made for me that first year and I'm certain I rarely even thanked her for doing it. Even looking back now, it's hard to fathom her willingness to go through all that during my first year at Meadowbrook. She was instrumental to my success and deserved a lot more acknowledgment and appreciation than she ever received.

Now set to begin my second year, I had even more motivation than the previous year as I desperately needed work to help erase all the pain I had been carrying due to the struggles at school. The shame I felt drove me like a madman, as I obsessively worked harder and put in more hours trying to prove to myself that I wasn't the loser I felt I had become. It paid off as mid-summer approached and I was promoted again, this time to *Honor Caddie*, the highest caddie rank at the club. With the promotion, I found myself regularly caddying for members who tipped very generously and I was starting to see a significant increase in the amount of money I was earning.

In addition to caddying, I was given an opportunity to work on staff at the First Tee facility as a Bagroom Attendant, a job which I happily accepted. The job responsibilities included washing golf carts, picking up golf balls at the driving range, and cleaning golf clubs. It didn't pay much but it kept me in the good graces of Jeff and his assistants. Between caddying and working at the First Tee, there were many days where I would get to work at six in the morning and not leave until nine or ten in the evening. I didn't mind the long hours because work was the only place I had any semblance of confidence, and that was a direct result of Jeff's strong presence in my life. His continued support helped to instill in me a sense of value and self-worth, both of which I never got at home and both of which I was starving for. By the end of my second year at Meadowbrook, I had eclipsed the number of rounds I had caddied the previous year and was flying high.

But summers always ended, and as the calendar crept closer to the start of my junior year, the fear and anxiety returned like old pals. I was terrified of going back to school, of going back to being a nobody, and eating lunch alone in that bathroom. I would not have survived one more lunch period in that prison and I was determined not to return to it. I don't know if it was the confidence Jeff had instilled in me or just dumb luck, but either way, when school began, there was no more eating lunch in the bathroom. My fears never materialized and I found myself eating lunch with students I'd met from class.

Missing the Mark

Although lunch was no longer a problem, focusing on my schoolwork and grades was another story. The first eight weeks of the year were tough academically, something that I had never experienced before. I showed little interest in school and neglected my studies, instead continuing work at the golf course after school and on the weekends. Work was the only thing I cared about and I never turned down an opportunity to put in more hours. Because of this, for the first time in my life, I was on the verge of failing a class. I was barely holding on to a D in AP History and, with only two weeks left in the quarter, there wasn't time to improve the grade. And in the house I grew up in, it would have been totally unacceptable to get a D on a report card. My parents expected, or - more accurately - demanded excellence from their children. My sisters and I were expected to be the best dressed, the best behaved, and of course, we needed to earn the best grades.

The pressure to excel in academics was a constant stress weighing on me. Even though I regularly earned A's and B's, something most parents would be proud of, it never felt good enough in a house where my three older sisters were consistently getting straight A's. My parents made school a competition, pitting my sisters and me against each other, seeing who would come home with the best grades. I couldn't compete with them and the result was that I often felt like the dumb one in the family. It was difficult growing up knowing I would never measure up to the high standards my parents had set and it often left me feeling like I was a disappointment to them.

So with the very real possibility of bringing home a D and the fear of the ramifications it would cause me at home, I made an appointment with my guidance counselor hoping to drop AP History and transfer into the standard History class. There was one problem though, and it was a big one: signing up for AP History meant you were locked into the class the entire first semester. You were not allowed to drop out of the class under any circumstances. So when I walked into my counselor's office, I knew the odds were stacked against me. She turned her chair around, looked up, took one look at my face and said:

"We are eight weeks in. You know that you can't drop this class, right?"

"I know, I know. But I'm behind in this class and there's no way I can improve my grade."

"No teacher is going to allow you to join their class with only two weeks left in the quarter."

I hadn't even sat down in her office, opting instead to stand before her with my hands clasped in a begging position - giving a long speech about how overwhelmed and desperate I was. She interrupted me with a raised hand. "Enough! I don't want to hear any more. If you can find another history teacher that will let you in their class this late in the quarter...I'll approve the transfer. But good luck finding that." She grabbed her notepad, wrote down a few words, tore off the piece of paper, then extended her hand towards me. She had written down a list of teachers who taught standard history. I wasn't out of the woods, but at least there was hope.

I spent the rest of the day visiting the teachers on the list and just like my counselor predicted, each one denied my transfer, one-by-one, until a single name remained on the paper—Mrs. Paquette. She was the only hope I had left.

I entered her classroom and there before me stood a middle-aged woman wearing thick glasses. Her straight brown hair was just long enough to touch the bright red shawl draped on her shoulders. I introduced myself and then began pleading with her as I explained my predicament. My story dragged on as I rambled about grades, my parents, pressure, work, and more and more until she interrupted me, let out a deep sigh and said, "Fine." She walked over to her desk, picked up a piece of paper, walked back, and handed it to me. "Be in class tomorrow and complete this assignment by Friday; it will be your grade for the quarter." At the time, the joy of erasing the D in AP History was all I cared about. But in hindsight, Mrs. Paquette's decision to allow the transfer did more than spare me from getting a D on my report card and quite possibly an ass-whipping at home. *It forever altered the trajectory of my life*.

Having dodged a bullet with AP History, I joined my new History class the following day. During that first class, I was approached by a student who introduced himself as Kal. Kal was one of just a few seniors in the class but he didn't exactly look like a typical high school student, at least none I had ever seen. His hair was heavily gelled. He wore a black leather jacket and a pair of Ray-Ban sunglasses. A few gold chains hung from his neck to match the gold ring and bracelet on his hand. Seemingly uninterested as to why I had joined the class so late in the quarter or even what my name was, his only question was if I was Middle Eastern. Not knowing where the conversation was going, I simply answered, "Yes."

"I am, too," he said. Then he pulled out a piece of paper from his notebook, wrote a number on it, and handed it to me. "Here's my pager number. Beep me after school and we can hang out."

Beepers and Babes

I had never called a pager before in my life and had no idea what he was talking about, but just like that, our friendship began with Kal giving me a quick lesson on how to use a pager. Soon after, we began hanging out. At first we hung out at places like the mall or his house, but that quickly changed. He began inviting me to house parties and then to a teenage dance club, both of which I had never experienced before. I was being introduced to Kal's friends at the pace of an uncontrollable wildfire. Before I knew it, most of his friends had become my friends and, let me tell you he had *a lot* of friends.

In addition to this new group of friends, I also began a friendship with another student from the new History class. Her name was Jessica and she was a member of the cheerleading squad. Jessica had straight blonde hair, blue eyes and a petite figure. She was absolutely beautiful and I loved being around her. Not only did we have a lot of fun together, but it boosted my self-esteem to be seen hanging out with such a pretty girl. Over time, Kal, Jessica and I became close friends and, one night, Kal and I decided to visit Jessica at work. She was working at Chuck-E-Cheese and, while we were there, Jessica introduced me to her co-worker, Stella, who was a short, dark-haired, curvy high school junior from another school district. I don't know what got into me but, by the end of the night, I was holding Stella's number in my hand. I had acted confidently, like a seasoned pro, but the truth is that was the first time I had *ever* had the courage to talk to a girl, let alone ask a girl for her number.

Over the next few weeks, as I learned more and more about Stella and her lifestyle, it was quite clear that she was a lot more aggressive than I was ready for. It wasn't long before I found myself in uncharted territory, when Stella began talking about sex and identifying herself as a "very sexual girl". She had been sexually active in her previous relationship and it was something she desired in ours. I had never even kissed a girl and was now needing to make decisions on whether or not to have sex at age 16. It hadn't been that long ago when I had no friends and ate in a school bathroom, and now suddenly I'm having to negotiate my virginity. I was surrounded by numerous friends, was being invited to house parties and dance clubs every weekend, and I even had a girlfriend — one who was not shy about her desire to have sex with me. How quickly things had changed.

When word spread within my new group of friends that I had the opportunity to have sex with Stella, many of them questioned why I hadn't yet taken advantage of the *benefits* being offered. I dodged the question as best I could, often giving vague answers to inquirers, simply noting that I wanted to wait to have sex. My answers never seemed to satisfy my friends and only fueled speculation that the real reason I wasn't having sex with Stella was because I was gay. For a while, that seemed to be the consensus of my friends and, although their assumption bothered me, I didn't feel like I could say much out of fear that these new friends would stop hanging out with me. And ultimately, I didn't feel the need to justify my stance on sex, especially since I had reservations on how they would react to a more detailed explanation for my choice to remain abstinent. The real reason I didn't have sex with Stella had nothing to do with wanting to wait.

Much like any teenage boy, my hormones were running wild and the temptation to have sex was there — especially with the open invitation right in front of me. But something happened early on while dating Stella that stopped me dead in my tracks. It's something I've never forgotten, even to this day. After experiencing my first dose of "messing around" with Stella and learning of her desire to have sex with me, I heard a voice. It wasn't an external voice speaking, but rather a gentle voice within me specifically telling me that I was not to have sex before I was married. It's important to note that I wasn't raised to think that you should only have sex when you get married. In fact, the extent of the birds and bees conversation with my dad was him saying, "You are my only son, I want you to be safe so make sure to use a condom." It was a 45-second conversation, and that was all. We never talked about sex again after that. So, to hear a voice telling me to wait until marriage was not the influence of my parents nor was it coming from my friends. And as I mentioned earlier, I didn't grow up in a religious home so that definitely had nothing to do with it. Not only was the voice very real and very clear, it spoke authoritatively, which compelled me to listen to it even though I didn't understand why or even *who* the voice belonged to.

Ultimately, the relationship with Stella didn't last. We had completely different personalities and I'm sure my decision to remain a virgin was probably a little more than she could handle. She got bored with me and soon moved on to greener pastures — starting with one of my new friends. The sadness of losing my first "girlfriend" was short-lived and soon forgotten as my new-found popularity clouded my mind, leaving memories of Stella far behind. The sheer number of people I could now call "friend" had exploded in such a way that my previous life was now almost unrecognizable. I was rarely home and quickly learning how to lie to my parents about where I was going and what I was doing. And when I was home, it wasn't for very long as I made a habit of sneaking out of my bedroom window to be out well past curfew.

I had somehow found myself on a fast-moving train, and the ride produced such a rush that I tolerated things I instinctively knew were wrong, all in the name of having friends. Over time, the darkness of this world and the temptations it brought drew me in deeper and deeper. I had been seduced by popularity and I pursed and worshipped it above everything else in my life. Popularity had become more than my addiction; it became my God.

CHAPTER 3

Promiscuous Virgin

Have you ever woken up and asked yourself, "How the hell did I end up here?" That question was on the tip of my tongue each day as I woke up in a world filled with nice cars and clothes, more friends than I could count, house parties, drinking, strip clubs, night clubs, underground raves and girls...lots and lots of girls. The details of the *when* and the *how* are foggy at best, but in a whirlwind...it happened. And in this new world, depravity defined almost every area of my life, and every form of temptation found its way onto the menu on a nightly basis. Popularity had a seducing effect and with every new experience, its claws held on tighter.

I'd graduated from the teenage dance clubs I was first introduced to in high school, moving on to the adult club scene, where there was a consistent obsession to go bigger and better every time. My friends and I had embarked on a never-ending tour of the dance club circuit. No exaggeration needed – we were literally in the clubs five to six nights a week and this went on for years. The club week began on Tuesdays for ladies' night at *Tiki Bob's*. We would go to *Have a Nice Day Café* on Wednesdays and Thursdays were spent at *Sneaky's*, a local club near my home in Canton. Friday nights were reserved for partying at *Clutch Cargo*s or we'd cross the border and party in Canada. Saturday nights were back in Canada at *Jokers* or *Don Cherry's* and by Sunday night, we finally made our way to downtown Detroit to party at *St. Andrew's Hall*.

This routine was exactly how each week played out for a couple of years, and it was exhilarating. I was addicted to the club scene and everything about it. The music, the dancing, and especially the girls. I loved the attention I received from being part of the "cool crowd". But more significantly, the club scene allowed me to be whoever I wanted to be. I was able to mask that insecure person I had always been, and could dress up and play the part of a confident person who was a popular, good-looking guy that could have any girl he wanted. And for the most part, I had everyone buying into my act. Over time, my friends and I became so well-known at the clubs that we were treated like VIPs. We'd often head straight inside, walking right past hundreds of would-be clubbers who were waiting in line. And once we were inside, that VIP treatment continued with the bartenders, who knew exactly what I wanted and had my drink ready for me every time I approached the bar. It was a powerful feeling.

Right or wrong, girls in the clubs noticed things like that, and I became a heck of a lot more attractive. Boy, did I love receiving constant attention from the scantily-clothed girls in the clubs, who were eager to throw themselves at me.

As the club scene became more and more lavish, the cost to stay a popular VIP increased as well. The more upscale clubs were filled with guys dressed in trendy clothes and what I had been wearing wasn't going to cut it anymore. An upgrade to my wardrobe was needed and I made it my mission to fill my closet with nothing but expensive, stylish clothes. And every time we were going to a "new" club or if there would be a new group of girls hanging out with us, I'd drop $200-300 on a new outfit just because I could. Not only did my clothes become more stylish but so did the cars I drove. The green Saturn I was so proud to have purchased on my own as a 17-year-old senior in high school was replaced at age 19 by a brand-new black Camaro fully loaded with T-Tops, leather, chrome rims, tinted windows and an expensive sound system. By age 21, the Camaro wasn't enough to turn heads so I leased a fully loaded black Lincoln LS—better suited for a middle-aged business man than a 21-year-old college student still living at home.

Although the image I was presenting to the world was one of confidence and borderline arrogance, I continued to struggle with who I was and where I belonged. The party persona had become my alter ego and the outward enjoyment I portrayed masqueraded my truth. I still felt the emptiness of that fifteen-year-old kid hiding in the bathroom. That emptiness was alive and well, and it was spreading like a disease consuming me from within. The same feelings that I battled in high school, the ones that told me I was ugly, not smart enough, not good enough and that I was unlovable...those feelings never really went away, no matter how hard I tried to let them go. All that really happened was that I learned to hide those inner demons better. Every time they would rise to the surface, I'd buy their temporary silence with another overpriced outfit or I'd go to the club and drop $100 buying drinks for friends or the pretty girls hanging around us.

Alcohol and Drugs

Throwing money around became my coping mechanism. It was also a façade that helped to momentarily cover up the truth, that there was nothing real about the smile on my face or the confidence I portrayed. I was experiencing everything but real joy. Nothing I bought or experienced erased the throbbing pain that lived just under the surface. And this was a burden that stayed with me every single day of my life. Everything in my life was superficial and I knew it, but it was all I had, and I felt trapped as I continued to hide the truth of just how lonely and depressed I was. And when buying things failed to give me what I needed, I looked for answers in a bottle. I significantly increased my alcohol use and became a hard-core binge drinker – consuming extraordinary amounts of alcohol to escape, albeit momentarily, from the sorrow lurking inside me. With my inhibitions gone, I was a constant fixture on the dance floor or, even worse, on top of speakers dancing with girls looking for attention. But every night and every buzz ends, and every morning I was still forced to face the reflection in the mirror. I still despised what I saw.

Around that time, the club drug Ecstasy was gaining a lot of popularity in the metro Detroit club scene. The allure of the drug and its promise of enhancing the user's senses and club experience appealed to me. I had contemplated trying it on several occasions, but I didn't know how to get my hands on it. A chance encounter would change all that. My friends and I were partying one night at a local strip club—one that we frequently visited. While there, I ran into someone I knew from the club scene, and while we chatted, I learned that he was on Ecstasy. He must have seen my eyes light up with interest, so he offered to sell me a few pills "for a good price". Deliberating the risks for what I was about to do lasted mere seconds and I left that encounter a few moments later with four Ecstasy pills in my pocket. I spent the rest of the night so giddy - much like a young school girl - over the illegal drugs in my pocket that I all but ignored my friends and the naked women dancing on stage.

Later that night, as I laid in bed staring at those blue pills, I felt a twinge of excitement. The idea of using drugs would never have been something to consider. But I was desperate to feel something inside, to fill whatever was still missing in my life and I suppose I thought drugs were the answer. Up to that point, I had never tried drugs, not even marijuana, and yet for some reason, I was not in the least bit worried about the potential dangers of this drug. Heck, I didn't even know the ingredients of Ecstasy, and I didn't care. The next day, I proudly showed off the pills to three of my closest friends and we made the decision to try it together that evening. But plans were interrupted and I was forced to bail on them last minute so they went ahead without me. The following day was filled with non-stop stories from my friends on how amazing the experience had been and I was left with nothing but regret for having missed out.

A few nights later, while hanging out in a pool hall with two other friends, talk of heading to a club entered the conversation. We eventually ditched billiards, and the three of us hopped in my car and headed for a club in Detroit. I still had the one remaining Ecstasy pill in my car and, eager to experience what my friends had, I threw caution to the wind and popped the pill while I drove. In retrospect, that decision seems awfully idiotic; but at that time, I was making poor choices left and right, and this one just added to that growing list. Within a few minutes of arriving at the club, I found myself in the middle of the dance floor surrounded by dozens of drunk girls. The effects of Ecstasy kicked in slowly, causing me to first become a little lightheaded. After that, things quickly spiraled out of control. My skin started burning and I began sweating profusely. The sexy girls I had been dancing with appeared to transform into demons, their beautiful faces turning death-like with fangs for teeth and horns coming out of their heads.

I stopped dancing to compose myself, though that only made things worse, as the entire dancefloor was now appearing to be surrounded by fire. I distinctly remember thinking the scene was what I would envision Hell to look and feel like. In my state of panic, I ran off the dance floor toward the staircase that lead to the basement, where the bathrooms were located. My heart was racing, the sweating uncontrollable, and my skin on fire as I sat alone on a bench near the restrooms. And if all that wasn't scary enough, the music played in slow motion, as if the DJ hadn't pushed the play button all the way down on his cassette tape.

In that state, everyone on my right appeared to be shrinking and melting into the ground, while everyone on my left appeared to be growing into giants and smashing into the ceiling. Capped off by the sound of a bell ringing in my ear, I was fearful that I had suffered permanent damage. Desperate for help on that bench, I sat there praying to God to rescue me from my self-inflicted dose of hell.

"Please God, get me out of this mess. If you make this all go away with no permanent damage, I promise I'll never try Ecstasy again."

I continued to whisper this prayer as my body went completely limp on that cold bench. By the time my friends had tracked me down, it was painfully obvious to them that I was tripping out from a bad high. They stood there trying to console me, but to no avail. I had sunk into full paranoia mode. My friends' continued efforts to calm me down were eventually interrupted by the sounds of a walkie-talkie and two paramedics lifting me up to my feet. One immediately flashed a light in my eyes and emphatically yelled, "Yeah, looks like he's on Ecstasy." I was unable to speak as I was forcefully dragged up the staircase and ushered into a private room near the front of the club. Although I could hear everything the paramedics were saying, I could do nothing more than sit there with my head face-down on the table. The female paramedic began taking my vitals while the male paramedic began asking me questions like what my name was, how old I was, where I lived and how many times I had tried Ecstasy. I tried explaining that it was the first time I had ever tried a drug but trying to give a coherent response proved difficult, as all my senses were out of sorts.

By this time, the female paramedic had finished taking my vitals and began yelling at me. I don't remember with absolute clarity everything she had to say, but she mentioned how kids died every day from taking drugs and that I was being stupid with my life. The male paramedic then asked why I had taken Ecstasy in the first place, and I told the truth – that I was curious. My answer enraged the female paramedic, who leaned over the table, got in my face, and yelled, "You know what curiosity did to the cat, right? It killed him!"

This exchange of words with the paramedic seems comical now; but, at the time, there wasn't the slightest bit of laughter in that room. She continued to berate me for several more minutes about the dangers of drugs and how many people she had seen die from overdoses. I was then informed that I was banned for life from the club and that if I ever returned I would be arrested for trespassing. I started to gain control of my body and was finally allowed to leave the room. The paramedics released me to my friends who had been forced to wait outside the room, but not before they instructed to take me to the emergency room if I exhibited any problems with breathing or consciousness.

We were then escorted out of the club and at the very moment I breathed in the cool evening air, I was hit with a jolt of energy. The hallucinating and drowsy effects of the drug seemed to immediately lift and an overwhelming carefree and euphoric feeling washed over me. I started flirting with a group of girls waiting to enter the club, which infuriated my friends who were still trying to make sense of the night's events. It took some time but my friends finally managed to get me back to the car. I sat shotgun as we drove back to the pool hall, all the while having to endure an exhausting lecture by my friends for putting them through their own version of hell. They couldn't understand how I went from looking like I was about to die in the club to being Mr. Congeniality in a matter of seconds. I didn't have an answer for them and truthfully, I didn't care. I spent the car ride trying to drown out their voices as I allowed myself to get lost in the hypnotic sounds of trance music playing from those expensive speakers. When we arrived back at the pool hall, I insisted I was fully functional and dismissed my friends' worries that I was incapable of driving myself home. I grabbed my keys, cranked up the music, sped away, and for the next few hours drove around aimlessly.

Alive but Still Dead

It was a little past 5 a.m. when I returned home and entered the family room through the garage door. To my surprise, my mom was sitting on the couch, drinking coffee and working on a crossword puzzle. I sat down on the couch across from her and let out a deep sigh.

"Late night?"

"Yeah, something like that."

"You don't look good. Are you drunk?"

"No. I promise I didn't drink tonight."

"Why do you look like that, then?"

"Um, well, I took Ecstasy."

"What is Ecstasy?"

"It's a club drug."

"I see".

During this brief exchange of words, my mom's posture on the couch never changed. She was still sipping on her coffee and seemed more focused on the crossword puzzle in her hand than on the topic of our conversation. Her eyes would peer up every few seconds and look my way, but there didn't really seem to be much of a reaction from her.

"Well, how did this drug thing work out?"

"Um, not so good."

I then proceeded to describe in detail the events of the evening, from the hell I went through in the club to needing assistance from paramedics to the euphoric feeling I felt driving around for hours before returning home.

"So...are you going to try this drug again?"

"Hell no! Those first twenty minutes scared the crap out of me. I thought I was going to die. The high after we left the club was amazing but, Mom, those first twenty minutes was literally like being in hell. I have never been so scared in my life."

"Well, I'm glad you learned from your mistake," she said before looking back down toward her puzzle. I sat there a little confused as to why there wasn't more of a reaction. I had just informed her that I thought I was going to die and needed medical assistance, and she was sitting trying to figure out the clues for three down and seven across. Unsure of what to say next, I got up from the couch, said goodnight then headed toward my room to sleep.

I kept my promise to God and never tried Ecstasy again, but the experience was a reality check of how much I was flirting with dangerous living. It was also an eye-opener because I soon began noticing that drug use was a lot more prevalent within my group of friends than I had realized. I began paying closer attention to my friends and learned that Ecstasy was heavily abused by many of them. Some even experimented with cocaine, mushrooms and whippets, but the drug of choice was by far marijuana. Several close friends began smoking it on a daily basis, and it slowly began creating friction within the circle of friends between those who smoked and those who didn't.

While drug use was definitely the darker side of our party scene and for the most part kept largely hush-hush, the sexual activity within the group was not. It was in excess and openly talked about on a daily basis. At times, it even seemed to be competitive in nature with many in the group trying to flaunt their sexual conquests. It's hard to pinpoint when it began or how it exploded the way it did; but, seemingly out of nowhere, sexual activity became a fixture on most night. It didn't matter where we were or what we were doing, girls were always around. And with an influx of willing females and the excess of alcohol and drugs—sex seemed to be on the mind of just about everyone. Being exposed to all that I saw awakened a desire inside that had been relatively dormant. Once I knew what it was, it was virtually impossible to shut off. And with each close encounter, the door opened wider and wider, and eventually, instead of just peeking in on the sexual activity, I was front and center, allowing myself to enter in. I witnessed many sexual acts first-hand, often from only a few feet away. The girls didn't care and often invited me to join in. I would be lying if I didn't admit that the desire to join was there...*always*. But the fear of potential consequences was always stronger. I was ashamed to watch but at the same time, there was a thrill to be around it.

Promiscuous sex had become so intimately woven into the group that it was not uncommon to be shooting pool or watching TV at a friend's house while sexual acts were going on twenty feet away. Sometimes these acts occurred behind closed doors, but often they were out in the open for all to see. It was also not uncommon to see threesomes occurring on the coffee table in the middle of someone's basement after a game of strip Euchre. Nor was it uncommon to find out that several friends had slept with the same girl...or groups of girls. There was no need to buy pornography – I had live shows going on right in front of me on a regular basis. And for the longest time, I had resisted the temptation to participate even though sex was in plain sight and freely offered to me by countless women on a regular basis. You see, that voice from years earlier that told me sex was reserved for marriage was still stuck in my head and it was as real as the day I heard it.

So I had remained a virgin and was determined to stay that way. But if you spend your time standing next to a pool, eventually, you're going to get wet even if you never jump in. The best intentions and self-restraint are no match for an environment overflowing with sex, which made it extremely difficult to stay *completely* pure. And while I did remain a virgin through it all, I eventually succumbed to lust inside me and began participating in certain sexual activities. I had become a promiscuous virgin.

CHAPTER 4

A House of Cards

I f you were to ask what my most painful memory is, the answer would require me to stretch far beyond one particular event. Sitting front-row watching two destructive addictions occur simultaneously cannot be adequately summarized in a single moment of pain, especially when the addicts were the two people I love most in this world: my mom and dad. And the catalyst was the opening of a casino in Windsor, just across the border between Detroit and Canada in the summer of 1998.

With no casinos in the Detroit area at the time, Canada became a hot spot destination for countless Michigan residents. My parents were no exception. I still remember the first time they decided to go, it was their own version of a "night on the town." My parents rarely went out and it was nice to see them doing something together. But not long after their first visit, they made another visit, and then another one. Soon after, they were regular patrons at the casino. But then the visits were no longer being made by my parents going together as a happy couple. Instead, my mom started going alone which was unusual because, for as long as I could remember, my mom had never been one to go out without my dad. As the intervals between my mom's visits to the casino got shorter and shorter - from once every few weeks, to every week, to several times a week - it was difficult to accept that my mom had fallen prey to what was an obvious and severe gambling problem. She was going to the casino almost every day after work, and coming home late into the evenings or early hours of the morning. I was in the midst of my own crazy party life, regularly coming home at two or three in the morning, and it was not uncommon for my mom and me to pull up in the driveway at the same time or within a few minutes of each other.

Just when I thought my mom's gambling couldn't get any worse, the casino exacerbated the problem when they began to comp her hotel rooms. How much money do you have to be losing for a casino to regularly hand you a free hotel room? And this led to a countless number of times where my mom would disappear and I wouldn't see or hear from her for days. During these episodes, I was forced to anxiously wait to hear from her, praying she was safe, but constantly wondering if she was even still alive. My mom's addiction was out of control and had escalated to a level where she was simply never home. I recall one August in particular where I tracked how many nights I went to bed without my mom being home. At the end of the month, there were twenty-seven marks on that calendar above my bed. Twenty-seven times out of the month that my mom was not home when I went to bed. Twenty-seven times that a college student living the club scene came home before his mom.

Money Out of Thin Air

Soon after, stories about my mom and her gambling became common occurrences. These stories were coming from all sides: my dad, extended family members, and even some of my friends who were all running into her at the casino. The stories ranged from her losing total control at the casino, betting more than she could afford, asking people for money, and lying about where she was going or how much she was losing. With all the stories I was hearing, I often wondered where the money was coming from. If she was losing as much money as people were saying, how could she continue to be at the casino every single day? The casino was not far from the clubs in Windsor that I was frequently visiting, so on occasion, my friends and I would stop by after the clubs closed so we could sober up before driving back home. They'd gamble while I searched for my mom. I don't recall a time when I stopped by the casino and she wasn't there. And when I would find her, she would have multiple stacks of $100 chips piled in front of her. I would see her tensely betting several hundreds of dollars per hand on blackjack. Her behavior was completely out of character.

This was not the mom I knew and loved; I was staring at a complete stranger.

My mom had been a homemaker for most of her life. It was only as my sisters and I got older that she began working at a bank. Until that point, my dad was the sole financial provider for a family of six. And while he didn't make a lot of money, we lived in a nice, three-bedroom, two-bathroom home. My parents were immigrants born in Ramallah, Palestine, a city not too far from Jerusalem, and both of their families moved to the U.S. in search of what most, if not all, immigrants search for – the American dream. With little importance put on education, my dad dropped out of school in 4th grade. So when he moved to the U.S. at the age eighteen, he worked several different jobs before eventually opening up his own tailor shop. Growing up, I was always proud of my parents. To me, they were successful. We may not have had a lot of money but my sisters and I were never in need; my mom made sure of that. My mom knew how to stretch a dollar, and so we always had new clothes, home-cooked meals on the table, birthday presents, and Christmas gifts under the tree. My parents went without so we kids didn't have to.

As time went on and business culture changed, with many companies shifting from a more professional look to something more casual, my dad's tailor shop started to suffer. The decrease in his income, coupled with the stress of my mom's addiction, added a tremendous amount of stress to the family. We simply didn't have the kind of money that could support the type of gambling problem that seemed to be going on. Knowing all of this caused me to regularly interrogate my mom about her expensive habit and her general erratic behavior. Our relationship began to splinter as she continually dodged my questions and did everything but provide me an honest answer about what was going on. There was always some elaborate story as to why she wasn't home, or why she didn't answer her cell phone for days at a time when I called. And she was always dismissive of her gambling or any notion that she had a problem. She would laugh it off, making me feel stupid for even insinuating such a thing. Her response was even worse whenever I questioned the amount of money she was gambling or anything related to how much money was being lost. I never thought it was possible to love someone so much while simultaneously hating them, but that's how I felt toward my mom. I could not trust my very own mother and my frustration with her prohibited me from enjoying any time with her or even having a healthy relationship with her. It seemed that every conversation ended with me blowing up at her and storming out of the house in anger over her addiction.

It took time, but I eventually found out where the money was coming from. It turned out that she had been using the cash advance option on several of her credit cards. And after maxing them out, she moved on to borrowing money from friends and family members. It seemed she owed money to everyone she knew — including her children. The gambling losses continued to mount, causing my mom to take even more desperate measures to fund her addiction. She began borrowing money any way she could, even if it meant using pawn shops and loan sharks.

Wins and Losses

Eventually, the gambling losses forced my parents to take drastic steps. They ended up refinancing their home, taking a heavy amount of equity out to pay off my mom's gambling debts. This broke my heart and fueled additional hatred toward my mom's reckless and uncontrolled behavior. Paying off the debt while not addressing the root issue – the addiction – was equivalent to putting a Band-Aid on a broken leg. I begged my dad not to go through with it, pleading with him and with anyone who would listen, but my words fell on deaf ears. Nobody was looking at the big picture: taking money out of the home was going to cause my parents to have a mortgage—one they were not going to be able to afford. Compound that with a tailor business that was beginning to fail, and it was clear as day that the road was going to lead to them losing their home. Neither my sisters nor my dad, and certainly not my mom, wanted to see the risk nor did they want to hear about it from me. I was shouting as loud as I could for someone to listen but nobody did. I was told I was being dramatic and exaggerating the severity of the problem. And in the end, the only thing refinancing the home did was delay the inevitable. With my mom's debt now wiped clean, she had a fresh slate to do it all over again – and she did.

As I had feared, my parents began struggling to pay the new mortgage. As things worsened, my dad realized the mistake he had made, and his regret, compounded with the stress of watching his wife deteriorate, led to a significant increase in his drinking. He was losing his wife, his house, his family, and he used the drinking to cope with watching everything he had worked for his whole life go down the drain. He was partially responsible for a lot of it, especially with his decision to refinance the home. But at the time, I'm sure he loved her and thought he was helping her. But she was an addict, and all the refinancing did was enable her. He didn't know how to cope and did the only thing he knew – and that was to drown his sorrows in a bottle.

There were so many nights that I'd find my dad so intoxicated on the recliner in the family room that it was hard to wake him up. When I would confront him about his drinking he would become violent and then shift the blame entirely on my mom. He'd yell about how it was her gambling that was causing him to drink, how he didn't have a wife anymore, how she had manipulated him to refinance the house and how she had ruined his life. And as my dad's anger increased, so did the drinking, which fueled even more fights between my parents. My dad's drinking would go deep into the night, and when my mom would return home from another all-nighter at the casino, all hell would break loose. The combination of two addicts merging, both fueled with hate for one another, consistently led to explosive arguments, many of which were physical in nature. I was often forced to restrain one or both of them and I can't even count how many times I was awakened in the middle of the night from their screaming or the sounds of shattering glass or breaking of dishes in the kitchen.

Everything in life had spiraled out of control and my mom's addiction was at the center of it. It was hard to accept that she had chosen the casino over her family, that she had chosen the casino over *me*. Add in her constant lying to me, her manipulation of reality and her seeming lack of concern for how her actions were affecting me, it was easy to see why she was on the receiving side of most of my anger. But she was still my mom and it left me in a tremendously vulnerable state. My heart was breaking for her and I could clearly see the damage she was causing herself, but getting her to see it was impossible. And what hurt the most was that I missed my mom – my real mom. Not the addict my mom had become, the one who consistently hurt me with lie after lie. No, I missed my mom who faithfully used to drive me to the golf course at 6 a.m. every morning. The mom who somehow always made ends meet no matter what. The mom who made miracles every birthday and Christmas to ensure my sisters and I always had new clothes, new toys, new everything. But those memories faded and gave way to the new reality that our once happy home was standing on a severely cracked foundation, and it was ready to give out.

As my mom's gambling losses once again piled up, I'd often find her coming home from the casino in the early hours of the morning, curled up on the couch crying. I'd try to console her while she'd be mumbling to herself about how much trouble she was in and how she owed money to "bad people". She'd beg me for money with promises that "this would be the last time". I'd succumb to feelings of guilt and fear that if I didn't give her the money she needed, these "bad people" would harm her. She would make promises to get what she wanted from me. Then she would break those promises and my heart, time and again. She'd be right back at the casino the very next night, doing it all over again. The addiction completely took over her. As much as I tried, my help wasn't enough for her. My money wasn't enough for her. And ultimately, *I* wasn't enough for her.

With the stress at home wearing on me, the party lifestyle I was living had begun to lose its appeal. But I hated being home so much that I felt forced to go out every night just to get away from the hell my home life had become. I barely slept, worked long hours, partied throughout the night, and I'd do it all over again the next day. I left almost no time for school and began skipping so much that I was constantly dropping classes because I was so behind. During this time I was still working at the golf course and, by then, had become an assistant manager. My role was to put on a smile and make sure the members received the best possible service each and every day. I loved the job but it was a challenge as it took every bit of energy in me pretending to be happy at work. The images of my mom curled up on the floor and crying about how she needed help with her addiction were burned into my brain. I was depressed and angry and I was on the verge of a complete meltdown. I had no idea what to do so I began to confide in Jeff about what was going on. I can't even begin to count how many times I sat in front of him crying about how dark things had gotten. The walls were closing in fast and I was barely holding on.

Betting Against Yourself

As my mom's gambling and my dad's drinking increased, so did my anger and bitterness. I could no longer function in a civil manner and every conversation with my parents resulted in a screaming match. Their behavior forced me to carry their addictions around, and I spent so much time worrying that I was becoming emotionally and physically ill. I hated their unwillingness to listen to any of my advice, I hated the way they both had become unreliable, and I hated all the lies they told me. And I hated them for how many promises they broke. I realize now that what I really hated was what the addictions had done to them. My parents had changed in ways that made them unrecognizable to me. It felt like I lost both of them, and it happened at a time when I needed them most. I was being swept away in a tide of my own reckless behavior and neither one even batted an eye. They completely failed to notice that my life was falling apart, and I resented them for it. Our relationship was so far beyond repair that I regularly wished that they would die. Imagine that, a child regularly wishing that both of his parents would die. And it was because I believed they brought absolutely no value to my life and if they were dead, they could no longer hurt me.

In late March of 2002, after yet another argument over my mom's gambling, I stormed out of the house, jumped in my car, cranked up the radio as loud as I could, and raced out of the neighborhood like a maniac. I drove around recklessly for hours. All my efforts to help my parents had failed, as did all my prayers to God and I couldn't understand why He was nowhere to be found all this time. My problems were real and they were severe and yet they didn't seem important enough to get God's attention. What was the point of God if he wasn't there to help, if he wasn't going to answer my prayers? I was on my knees almost every night crying, begging for help, and his silence fueled a complete and utter disdain for Him.

While venting my frustrations through the reckless driving, I happened to pass an apartment complex with a "Now Leasing" sign on the curb. Almost instinctively, I made a U-turn and drove to the leasing center for the Village Squire Apartments. Without even thinking it through, I walked in and filled out an application. The leasing lady tried to sell me on all the great amenities, but I had no interest in what she had to say, nor did I care about the square footage, what the apartment looked like, or if there was new carpet. I just wanted out of my parent's house and I wanted out that day! I knew that financially I couldn't afford moving out, but emotionally, I knew that I couldn't afford to stay at my parent's house any longer. After filling out all the paperwork, I was approved on the spot and, just like that, I was moving out.

When I returned home later that day, there was an uneasiness flowing inside me. I remember sitting on the couch in the family room watching my mom cooking in the kitchen. She looked at me in that way all mothers do when they know something is up. She knew there was something on my mind.

"What's going on?"

I didn't know the best approach and didn't even try to polish up the words. I simply blurted out, "I got an apartment, I'm moving out." Her face seemed puzzled but she seemingly shrugged it off as if it was some kind of joke. "No, Mom, I'm serious! I signed a lease today. I move out tomorrow."

"What?! What do you mean, honey? Why? Don't move out." Her concern was too little, too late.

"What do I *mean*? Are you kidding? I hate living here. I hate you and I hate Dad! I don't want to live in this hell anymore!" I had made my decision and there was no turning back. I was about to pay a very high price for peace, but the cost was worth it.

CHAPTER 5

Amanda

With neither of my parents home, I made one last trip to box up the few remaining items still there. After completely cleaning out my bedroom, I stood in the hallway taking in one final look. It dawned on me that the good times I had experienced in the only home I had ever known now seemed so distant, almost impossible to remember. The memories of playing catch in the backyard with my dad during the summer months and watching movies in the family room with my mom and sisters on Friday nights as kids had all but been erased. What now filled the home was an overwhelming heaviness in the air, a sadness over the loss of both my parents to their addictions. And with the addictions came the lies, the fights, and the chaos. So many mistakes and so many regrets. There were so many opportunities to stop all of this but one bad decision after the next had left my relationship with my parents fractured and beyond repair. It should never have come to this, but it had. And I no longer had the energy or the desire to try and mend it.

My reminiscing was suddenly interrupted as the sound of my cell phone cut through the silence of the empty house.

"Hello?"

"Hey, it's me, Amanda. Can we talk?"

I paused as my heart dropped with apprehension.

"I'm at my parents' house getting ready to leave; can I call you back in five minutes?"

"I know. I'm parked out front."

Shock filled every fiber of my being as I cautiously opened the front door thinking this was some kind of joke. But sure enough, parked on the street was Amanda's silver Pontiac Grand Am. From just those few seconds of talking to her, a whirlwind of emotions swept through my entire body. It had been a long time since I had last spoken to Amanda and I needed to process her unexpected visit. After I composed myself, I put my belongings in my car and then headed toward hers. I approached from the passenger side and leaned in through the open window. Amanda spoke first.

"Hey. I was hoping we could talk."

"I would invite you inside, but I don't live here anymore."

"I know. I've been driving by a lot lately but haven't been seeing your car."

"I just moved into an apartment not too far from here. If you want, you can follow me and we can talk there. Would that be okay?"

She accepted the invitation and as I pulled out of the driveway, I watched in the rearview mirror as she followed close behind. My apartment was nearby; but that night, the five minute drive felt like an eternity as a wave of memories raced through my mind. Amanda was the biggest regret of my life.

I met Amanda on a chilly August night the summer after graduating high school. That night, my friends and I were hanging out in downtown Plymouth when four cute girls approached us. They recognized my friend Daniel from school, and after a few introductions, we stood around chatting for a bit. There was an innocence about Amanda as she stood there surrounded by an almost angelic glow. She was this cute, skinny girl with straight, dark brown hair, wearing a white and purple jacket. After a few minutes of playful flirting, the girls went their way and my friends and I went our way. The next day, I returned home from work to a message on the answering machine:

"Hi, this is Amanda. We met last night. Daniel gave me your phone number and said it would be okay to call you. If you're interested in getting to know each other, give me a call."

I wish I could have played it cool and waited a few days before calling her back. I didn't. I couldn't. I was too excited. When I called her back that night, our conversation lasted six hours. The topics we covered shifted back and forth between deep and heartfelt to playful banter. She was funny and easy to talk to. There was also a purity to her words mixed in with a level of maturity that was undeniable. I adored Amanda and immediately knew there was something special about her. I also felt exposed while talking to her. She had a way of penetrating into the depths of my soul. She saw me, the real me, and understood me in a way that nobody ever had. The dialogue never went stale, progressing naturally, flowing perfectly from one topic to the next. Before our phones died, we agreed to go out on a date, and a few nights later I was standing on her mom's front porch picking her up.

There was nothing overly memorable about our first date except the conversation. The verbal chemistry we began during the initial call continued, right up to the point when I learned Amanda's age. She was about to begin her sophomore year of high school and was a few months shy of her sixteenth birthday. I, on the other hand, was eighteen and a freshman in college. The age difference felt wrong, but Amanda demeanor and maturity was years ahead of a typical fifteen-year-old. So, against my better judgement, I resisted my inclination to end things and we agreed to go out again. We had our second date a week later and this time, we decided to double date with Amanda's best friend Rebekah and her boyfriend Simon. After dinner, Rebekah invited all of us back to her mom's house where we were greeted in the driveway by Rebekah's older sister, Abby. Rebekah introduced me to Abby and from the first moment I laid eyes on her, I immediately felt a spark between the two of us. I spent the rest of the evening hanging out with Rebekah, Simon and Amanda upstairs in Rebekah's room; but my mind was on Abby, her olive skin and her curvy but petite frame. The drive home that night felt especially long. I was torn between the amazing emotional and verbal chemistry I had with Amanda and the physical attraction I felt toward Abby.

How to Lose a Girl in 5 Minutes

Eighteen-year-old boys seldom think logically, especially when it comes to girls, and I was no exception. The next day I called up Daniel looking for information on Abby's relationship status. He let me know she was single and offered to see if she would be interested in going out with me. And just like that, the wheels were in motion. But there was a problem – Abby went to the same school with Rebekah, Amanda, and Daniel. And acts of betrayal don't stay secret for long, especially not in high school. It wasn't long before Amanda found out that I was inquiring about Abby and it broke her heart. Soon after I was confronted by Simon who shared how distraught Amanda was. I tried to wash away my sins by using her age as a legitimate reason for what I had done, but there was no excuse. Nothing I could say was going to justify my actions, and the effects of this mistake would have long-lasting consequences.

After breaking Amanda's heart, I did everything I could to make Abby my girlfriend, investing an unbelievable amount of time, energy, and money into the chase. And, oh, how I chased this girl. I did everything for her. I took her everywhere and I paid for everything. I pulled all-nighters helping her study or doing her homework *for* her. I gave her comfort and support, and did everything a boyfriend should do, except…I wasn't her boyfriend. I never managed to get out of the friend zone with her, as Abby simply could never let go of her abusive, drug-addicted ex-boyfriend. But she knew I liked her and she used that to her advantage. She strung me along, keeping me close enough that I wouldn't date other girls, but was never willing to commit to me. And in the end, it all blew up in my face.

Ultimately, I got played by Abby and in a way, I suppose it was poetic justice for what I had done to Amanda. But interestingly, during the entire time I pursued Abby, I ran into Amanda dozens upon dozens of times, often in very random places. Every time we'd see each other, regret would rise up in the pit of my stomach. I knew I had screwed up with her, but I was too ashamed to admit it to her. Not to mention that my pride didn't allow me to accept defeat in my pursuit of Abby. Had I been smarter, I would have run back to Amanda, hat in hand, and she would have probably taken me back. But instead, I kept quiet and never spoke all the words I should've said. To her credit, Amanda was always pleasant when we saw each other. She also never discussed to what degree she knew about my involvement with Abby, although I suppose Rebekah would have filled her in since I was at Abby and Rebekah's mom's house all the time. Either way, she never brought it up and she never dished out any harsh criticism my way, even though I rightly deserved to be called out for treating her poorly. Instead, every time we saw each other the two of us would pick right back up with our playful banter and flirty conversations, some of which lasted for several hours at a time.

When I met Amanda at age 15, she was a cute girl. But a few years later, she had blossomed into a gorgeous woman. She was absolutely stunning. Her beauty took my breath away each and every time I would run into her and that only intensified the regret I harbored inside. I secretly held on to hope that I would somehow, someday, get a second chance with her. That dream ended the night one of Amanda's friends approached me at a club. She told me with absolute delight that Amanda had gotten engaged. The news sent me into a downward spiral and I proceeded to down shot after shot before hopping in my car and making the 45-minute drive home completely intoxicated. It's still a mystery how I didn't end up in jail or the morgue that night.

All these thoughts were swirling in my head as I pulled into my apartment complex with Amanda driving right behind. We parked, exited our cars, and made our way through the common entrance door and up the stairs to my second-floor apartment. Once inside, I led Amanda to the family room and to the black leather couches that had been delivered that morning. But before either of us had a chance to sit down, Amanda blurted out those dreaded words, "I'm engaged."

Standing there blank-faced, I was too stunned to say a word. I had known she was engaged for a while but hearing her say it in person was a gut punch. Was that the purpose of her needing to talk to me? Did she want to break my heart in person and finally get revenge for what I had done to her years ago? But before I could even respond, Amanda continued, "I don't know if I can marry him. Every time I think about my future, about kids, the white picket fence, you are the one I see in those dreams. I can't stop thinking that maybe we were meant to be. Every time I try to move on with somebody else, I keep thinking we didn't try hard enough. I've had this bottled up in me for a while. Every time I run into you in some random place, I want to say something but I'm too afraid. And we seem to run into each other all the time. It can't just be a *coincidence*, can it?"

I was speechless. Where was all this coming from? Here I thought she was trying to break my heart but instead, perhaps she was going to be the one to fix it. Was

I finally going to get my second chance with Amanda? There was so much hurt in my personal life with my parents' addiction. Now, all of a sudden, it seemed like Amanda could be my hope for salvation and that she would heal everything that was broken inside of me. Throughout the years, I had continued to believe we'd eventually be together. In my mind it made perfect sense. Our natural chemistry had never faded and the desire to be with her increased with every conversation we shared over the years. We were constantly running into each other. Between the clubs, the pool halls, crossing the border into Canada...she was always standing in front of me. Not to mention that there was always this unspoken connection between us, and now, she was standing in my apartment, telling me she thought I was the one for her. I had tried to fill the void inside me with years of partying and drinking. I had tried filling it with many close encounters of sexual promiscuity with random girls I met in the clubs and at parties. But nothing had worked. Amanda's presence was a ray of light in the darkness that had become my world. Her words that night melted my heart and the concrete wall I had built around it.

We eventually got around to sitting on the couch and, as I looked into those beautiful, sparkling eyes, I let her know I had never stopped caring about her and that I had always thought about a future with her as well. The two of us on that couch felt perfect as we talked all night, just like we had on so many occasions over the years —

only this time, it was different. It felt like the beginning of a new life.

Joy and hope had been missing for years, and it wasn't a coincidence they returned the moment she did. The timing couldn't have been more perfect. I was free from the dysfunction at my parents' house and now the girl who might actually be the one for me had professed that I might be the one for her. It was the life I had always wanted, the one I felt I deserved, and it was finally happening.

Effortlessly and seemingly overnight, it appeared the two of us were heading down the road of becoming the couple we were always meant to be. Amanda soon began coming over to my new apartment regularly. One night, with the windows open, we were enjoying a beautiful breeze and a warmer than normal April evening. We laid close to each other, laughing, talking and kissing while soft music played in the background. As the talking turned into yawns, we called it a night and I escorted Amanda to her car. Before saying goodnight, we embraced for the longest, most passionate, most intimate kiss we had ever shared. I didn't know that this perfect kiss would also be our last.

The next morning I was awakened by the alarm clock and not Amanda. It hadn't been long since we had reconnected, but I had gotten so used to her early morning calls that not hearing her voice first thing in the morning was disappointing. That disappointment turned into concern when I called her on the way to school and got her voicemail. After leaving a message, I spent the rest of the day obsessively checking my phone, anxiously waiting for her call. With each hour that passed and no returned call, my mind spiraled into a world of worry and insecurity. It seemed like I spent most of my life in a constant state of preparing for the worst, always expecting the bottom to fall out, and that day was no different. My emotions were all over the place as I formulated a hundred reasons for Amanda's disappearance. It was not until late that evening that Amanda finally returned my call and confirmed the fears I had been carrying around all day. The quiver in her voice as she began to speak resonated into the deepest part of my soul.

"I'm sorry, but I can't. I just can't do this. I'm sorry."

"What do you mean?" I was completely caught off guard by what I was hearing. "What about all those things you said to me the other day? The white picket fence, your dreams, our future?"

And then came the explanation.

"I know you're the one for me, but I'm afraid you'll wake up one day and want someone better than me. Hearing that would break my heart and I don't want to go through that. I would rather not try and regret it for the rest of my life than to try and have it not work out. I don't want to know that I wasn't enough for you."

At the time, I thought it was fear in her voice but it wasn't. It was hurt. I had wounded her so badly in the past and never made it right. I never made her feel safe and secure with my feelings for her. I never owned up to the mistake I had made nor had I ever made the effort to assure her it would never happen again. In the rush to reconnect with her, I had quickly glossed over her pain without even considering the possibility of a lingering hurt still lurking deep inside her.

I didn't say much for the remainder of that call. I just sat there at the dining room table, trying to digest Amanda's words. We had spent several days talking about how perfect the future was going to be, but the reality was that we were never going to be able to live up to the expectations of our dreams. Amanda realized it. Maybe she was right, but it still stung like hell. We were so close to making it happen, but this was as far as the road would take us. The dreams we had been building up in our heads for years were now lying in rubble before us. The call was short and, when it ended, I sat at the dining room table, numb and unable to move. After what seemed like hours of sitting there in silence staring at the wall, I looked down at my phone to check the time, but it was the date that burnt in my mind: April 21 – my parents' anniversary. A date that brought nothing but bad memories as my parents' marriage had pretty much disintegrated. My disgust over the date was palpable. I couldn't help but think in that moment that God had a dark sense of humor. Why would He allow me to see Amanda again, only to have the relationship crash and burn in the way that it had. And on this particular date of all things.

It was as if God were deliberately putting a big bold exclamation point on my pain while simultaneously letting me know that He could do whatever the hell He felt like doing, whenever He felt like doing it! I resented God for allowing it and I let Him know it as I unleashed all my anger toward Him. After unloading all my emotions at God, I mustered up what was left of my energy and headed toward the bedroom. As I crossed the family room, I stopped and stared at the black leather couches. 24 hours earlier those couches were the scene of Amanda and me tightly embracing while we exchanged intimate kisses. The couches were now empty and the apartment felt cold. Without Amanda, everything in my world felt cold.

CHAPTER 6

Blurred Vision

The voices in my head reminding me I wasn't good enough, that I had no value and that I would never be loved by anyone, was a battle that continued to rage on. Regardless of the season of life I was in, or the popularity I had experienced, this self-doubt was a nagging voice that simply wouldn't go away. The fallout of Amanda's departure and the way it happened seemed to give these voices more credibility and more power over my life. And whatever air was left in my world was sucked out and I began to suffocate under the weight of my misery. For a while, it was hard to know who I hated more, Amanda or God, as each seemed equally responsible for all that was wrong with me.

The benefit of living alone afforded me the opportunity to drink the voices away, an attempt that proved futile; I couldn't drink enough beer to escape the loneliness. And trust me, I gave it my best effort. Most nights ended with a drunk version of me kneeling down at my bedside begging God for help. It didn't matter how authentic my prayers were—nothing seemed to move God's heart, and He continued to ignore me. That was by far the hardest hurt to accept. I expected humans to treat me poorly, but God? It went against everything I had ever heard about Him. God was supposed to be good, wasn't He? God was supposed to be loving, but was He? He appeared to be anything but those things and His distant, apathetic approach toward my hurts seemed more vengeful than compassionate.

With my faith waning and my frustrations toward God reaching explosive levels, I opened myself up to the opinions of those around me—opinions I would have previously never allowed to take root. One viewpoint that seemed to rise to the forefront was atheism, a seed that had been planted by my friend JP. While not really a constant fixture in my circle of friends, JP had at one time been one of my closest friends. He was also one of the very first friends I met five years earlier at the beginning of the popularity explosion. We had drifted apart over the years, not because of any particular fallout, but simply because we chose different paths at the fork in the road. He chose higher education and the pursuit of his master's degree, while I chose the path of partying, clubs and chaos.

Over the years, we hung out on a few occasions, but he mostly remained on the fringes of my social circle. What I didn't know until we reconnected for a longer conversation one particular night was that he had walked away from his upbringing and belief in God. He ditched his Christian roots and had become an atheist. After listening to me talk about all that was wrong in my life and my frustration with God's silence, JP chimed in with what he believed to be the most logical explanation. JP concluded the reason God was silent was not because He was mad at me, but rather, *because there was no God at all.*

Growing up, I remember hearing the word "atheist" and always connecting it to "bad people" who were destined to go to Hell. But JP was a good friend, an intelligent guy. He was well-read and one of the smartest guys I knew. He was also someone that seemed to have a great amount of faith prior to his recent conversion to atheism. So curiosity prompted me to learn more about his views and why they had changed so drastically. JP gave a compelling argument, which was largely based on what he called "scientific evidence". And so I left the conversation that night open to the possibility that maybe JP was right that God didn't exist. What stuck in my head most was a no-God scenario would allow me to discard the anger and frustration that had been building up toward God's seemingly terrible track record with me. It would also allow me to discard the guilt I was carrying for not being good enough to please God.

If there were a God, He was a God that allowed me to be verbally and emotionally abused by my parents growing up. He allowed me to be so desperate that I was forced to eat in a bathroom for months during high school. He allowed me to become so popular only to learn that popularity and partying couldn't fill the emptiness inside me. He allowed both of my parents to become addicts during the years I needed them the most. And as if all that weren't enough, He allowed Amanda to come out of nowhere to fill my head and heart with ideas of everlasting love only to watch it be taken away. It just seemed that either God was terrible at being God or He didn't exist. The jury was still out but JP's argument against God's existence had an alluring appeal and it was something I couldn't easily dismiss.

Stranger Things

A few nights later after this eye-opening debate on God's existence, I was out late with friends at a local bar. As I drove home after a long night of drinking, I stopped at the Speedway gas station near my apartment. While walking back to my car, a speeding green Infinity pulled up in front of me, nearly running me over. The car parked, and out came Sam and Ronnie – two guys I had known casually from the club scene. I wouldn't necessarily call us friends, but we knew a lot of the same people and had hung out on a few occasions over the years. They approached me and we spent a few minutes catching up. As the brief conversation was winding down, a loud noise that sounded like metal scraping concrete caught our attention. The three of us looked in the direction of the noise and from behind the bushes that lined the outskirts of the parking lot, an older blue car emerged, struggling to make its way into the parking lot. The car had obviously been in an accident of some kind because the passenger side was severely damaged near the front of the vehicle and it appeared the tire could fall off at any second. That obnoxious noise we were hearing was the car's metal frame dragging on the concrete. When the car finally parked, a couple of teenagers rushed out to survey the damage. The entire scene was somewhat comical, and the three of us enjoyed a few laughs at the expense of these young kids.

As the scene continued to unravel before our eyes, I made a comment about how my night had been crazy when Sam chimed in: "Man, this whole day has been crazy. I got into an argument with my uncle earlier. I work at his restaurant and he accused me of stealing today. I can't believe my own uncle would think that about me. Now I'm having issues with my mom because she's in the middle of it. Do me a favor, please don't repeat what I just said to anyone. I don't want people knowing my business."

I nodded, letting him know I understood his request. Sam then mentioned that he and Ronnie were on their way to get something to eat and extended an invitation to join. I politely declined as it was almost two in the morning and I had to be at work at 6:30 a.m. As I walked to my car, Ronnie's Infinity pulled up next to me with Sam's head sticking out of the passenger window.

"You sure you don't want to join us? Come on. Get in your car and follow us."

I figured what the hell. What was another night of no sleep? It wasn't like I hadn't been doing that nonstop for the past several years. The two of them sped off and I followed close behind for a couple of miles until we reached the Denny's restaurant near the highway, a frequent final destination after most of my nights out.

The restaurant was quiet when we arrived, the calm before the 2 a.m. bar rush. We were escorted by the hostess toward the back where I noticed Matthew, a longtime friend of mine, sitting in a large booth with a guy I didn't recognize. He noticed me as well and invited me, Ronnie and Sam to join him and his friend. As the five of us sat together, we began to exchange stories about what we'd been up to that evening. We shared a few laughs and engaged in a handful of "remember when" stories until we eventually landed on an odd topic. I don't recall how or why but the conversation had shifted toward discussing a previous close friend of mine, a guy by the name of Charlie.

Imagine a muscular nineteen-year-old with heavily gelled hair slicked back, wearing a white tank top, baggy jeans and several gold chains, full of arrogance and an undeniable swagger in his walk. That was the first impression I had of Charlie, whom I also met through Kal five years earlier, a few months after Kal had introduced me to JP and Matthew. Charlie and I instantly bonded. Like me, Charlie was heavy into the club scene, and for the first few years of our friendship, that's all we ever did —

spend all our nights in the clubs. However, as time went on, Charlie and I began to drift apart. I loved hanging out with him but he was extremely difficult to be around because his energy level was uncontrollable and his need to be constantly intoxicated made him the type of person you could love and hate hanging out with, all at the same time. A heavy drinker who had been seduced by the euphoric pleasures of Ecstasy, Charlie was both an alcoholic and a drug addict.

It had been quite a long time, perhaps as much as a year, since I had last seen Charlie, and during that time I had heard plenty of stories about how he had become extremely religious. But his new-found faith went far beyond church attendance or talking about God. The rumors circulating were that he had been given a kind of power from God where he would get visions about people, either about what had already happened to them or things that were going to happen. There was even a story going around that he claimed to have seen angels floating all around. Hearing something like that was hard to comprehend for those of us who knew him because Charlie's character didn't fit nicely into what most people would associate with a religious person. He was either drunk or high just about any time you'd run into him and he didn't exhibit many godly characteristics.

So on this particular night, Sam, Ronnie, Matthew, Matthew's friend, and I sat in a corner booth at Denny's engaged in a lengthy conversation about Charlie, his new found religion, and the power he supposedly had. The night went on and the stories about Charlie continued, with each story more fantastical than the previous one until, out of nowhere, my ears perked up to a familiar voice coming from the front of the restaurant. To my surprise, Charlie was standing at the entrance. What were the odds of him showing up well after 2 a.m., all alone and at the same restaurant that all of us were sitting at, at the exact same time we were talking about him?

Seeing Things

At the time, it was easy to chalk it up to simply being a *coincidence* but that wouldn't turn out to be the case. When Charlie's eyes caught mine, he headed straight to the table and forced himself into the booth we were already tightly packed into. We had been talking about Charlie and his "visions" for quite some time, and now he was sitting in our midst. The night continued down a path of strange events, as all of our separate evenings had now intersected, culminating in a corner booth at the back end of a Denny's restaurant.

From the moment Charlie sat down, he was in his typical verbal overdrive. His topics were all over the place – clubs, drinking, girls – with random statements about God mixed in for good measure. If anything, he was the antithesis of a godly man and my long history with Charlie prohibited me from being able to take anything he said seriously. Charlie was definitely intoxicated that night so it came as a surprise that he noticed a few of us were taking subtle jabs at him. My poker face must have been off because once Charlie clued in and noticed I was speaking poorly of him and perhaps his God, his demeanor completely changed.

He locked eyes with me and said, "Yeah, laugh now, but wait until God shows you all the things He's going to show you. Wait until you see what God is going to do in your life."

He said it in a manner that I had never heard him use—in such an authoritative and confident way. He continued with, "Just wait, see how God uses you. You laugh now, and you're going to go through some hard times over the next couple of years, but God is going to use these things to save you." After scolding me, he looked around at the others and blurted out, "Who got into a car accident tonight?" We all just stared at him. When nobody responded he spoke again, "The passenger side of the car, with the messed up tire. Maybe not your cars, but earlier tonight there was a blue car all banged up?" Sam, Ronnie and I looked at each other, surely thinking the same thing: *how could he have known?*

Ronnie responded first, "How'd you know that?"

Charlie casually responded, "See, you all laugh about God. You see. I told you God gives me visions."

The rest of us at the table were at odds trying to explain how Charlie knew about the car, but I'm sure we all thought the same thing, that it was just a *coincidence*. But then Charlie turned to Sam, "That issue with your mom and your uncle at the restaurant, don't worry about it, it's all going to work itself out." Sam sat up straight in the booth, clearly startled by what he had just heard and asked Charlie to clarify what he meant. "Is there something going on with your mom, like your uncle thinks you're stealing from the restaurant and now your mom is mad at you?" Sam angrily turned his head in my direction in such a way to insinuate I had somehow told Charlie what he had shared with me earlier in the evening at the gas station. In Sam's defense, I would have been the likely culprit, seeing how his options were that either Ronnie or I spoke to Charlie about that private conversation. And since Sam was with Ronnie in the car ride to Denny's, that left me as the one without an alibi. I made Sam and the rest of the table very much aware that not only did I not tell Charlie anything, I didn't even have his number. I looked to Charlie to corroborate my story, which he did. Then he proceeded to tell Sam that it was God who told him what had happened.

At that point, Matthew, who was unaware of everything that had happened at the gas station before our arrival at Denny's, asked what everyone was talking about, to which Sam reluctantly explained. In a lawyer-like manner, Matthew began questioning every detail of the story and every person involved, trying to uncover a potential loophole to how Charlie knew what he knew. This continued for several minutes, but the problem with Matthew's line of thinking was that there were no reasonable lines to draw between Charlie, Sam and the story. The temperature and mood at the table quickly changed and we sat at Denny's for the next few hours interrogating Charlie and dissecting every comment he made like we were detectives trying to crack a cold case file.

No one was satisfied with Charlie's explanation that God was giving him visions, especially me. To hear that God was regularly speaking to Charlie and giving him visions, someone who I looked at as being inferior to me, was a slap in the face. Charlie is an addict and gets visions from God, and here I am, a good person, and I can't even get God to answer one single prayer? I wanted to find resolution, but it was already past 5 a.m. I had no choice - I needed to get home, shower, and get ready for work. I left Denny's, but not before I exchanged numbers with Charlie.

On my drive home, I replayed the night over and over in my head but couldn't shake it. What had I just witnessed? There were far too many coincidences that had occurred for the night to have gone the way it had. From the gas station to Charlie demonstrating his God-like power, the whole night had been a frenzy. There had to be a logical answer, but I couldn't find one. Several days later,

I was still racking my brain, so I called up Charlie and invited him over.

Child's Play

He came over that evening and I tried to engage him in a serious talk about God though that was easier said than done. His attention span was short and the conversation went nowhere. Over the next few weeks, I continued to invite him over for additional discussions, which continually tested my patience. At times, hanging out with him could be the most entertaining thing but it could also drive a person absolutely crazy because Charlie is like a distracted toddler, unable to stand still for even a few minutes when he's drinking or on drugs. And whenever he came over, he was always either drunk or on drugs, many times both. Throughout the course of the evenings, as he would become more and more intoxicated, the spilling of his drink on the counters, the carpet, and the couches increased, as did my impatience and frustration toward him. I'd constantly find myself cleaning up after him as if I were his maid. Charlie's antics had me constantly questioning if hanging out with him was worth the trouble. But I needed answers to what I had seen him do at Denny's, so I was left with no other choice but to indulge him and his erratic behavior.

After several weeks and numerous attempts, Charlie finally got around to explaining what it meant to not only believe in God but to actually know him. Charlie talked about Jesus, the cross, as well as how a person needed to surrender their life to Jesus to be saved. He would often mention being "born again" and how I needed to be born again to be a child of God. It was a lot to process, and going back to God for help was the last thing I wanted to think about, let alone do. God had let me down too many times and I didn't think I could trust Him again.

I was also still weighing JP's atheistic view and was perhaps leaning that way more and more. It was hard to trust God. He reminded me so much of everyone around me who was absolutely unreliable, especially my parents. His promises were empty. What use was a God whom you couldn't see, couldn't hear, and couldn't talk to? One who demanded our commitment to Him but was not willing to offer the same in return? But what was I to make of the night at Denny's and how Charlie knew about the damaged blue car in the parking lot, about Sam's family issues, and all the rest? And that night was far from the only time Charlie freaked me out with those "visions" from God. They became a regular occurrence when hanging out with Charlie.

Charlie and I had gone to a nightclub called Tonic in Pontiac. I was getting tired, so we left a little earlier than normal. As we made our way to the parking lot Charlie blurted out, "We are going to witness tonight." I asked what that meant and he explained that he was having a vision of talking about Jesus to two Muslim guys. Even though we were the only two people in the parking lot, I firmly requested that he not talk to any Muslims about

Jesus because I didn't want to bring unnecessary problems our way after a long night of drinking. Not to mention that I knew many Muslims and my experience had been that they were often very devout in their faith and wouldn't take a conversation about abandoning their beliefs in Islam for Christianity very well.

As we neared my car, two men approached us in need of help since their car battery had died. They asked for a jump and I was happy to assist. I drove my car near theirs and while one of the guys began connecting the cables, two other men happened to walk by and asked if the four of us needed help. Before anyone could respond, Charlie looked at the man offering help and told him he should take the new job he was just offered. The man looked puzzled and asked Charlie what he meant. I watched and listened carefully as Charlie told this man that his current job was a dead end and that his boss was holding him back. He then added that the new job offer would turn into his dream of becoming a head chef. Charlie had clearly hit a chord with this guy because his face reflected his complete shock. He asked Charlie how he knew everything he had just said and Charlie stated that Jesus had given him a vision.

The man went on to tell the group of us that he hated his job as a cook and that he had received a job offer the previous day but was afraid to accept it because he had been at his current job for a very long time. Charlie continued to encourage him, letting him know that he shouldn't be afraid and that the new job was going to be a great move for him. The man and his friend walked away, clearly very freaked out by what had just happened. When we turned back to the two original men who were working on the cables and jumping the car battery, they were staring at Charlie in awe. One of them asked Charlie who Jesus was and the next thing I knew, Charlie was talking to these men about Jesus and the Bible. And the craziest part of the story is that it turned out that these two men were Muslims. I don't know if those men ever converted to Christianity but the fact that Charlie had predicted that he was going to witness to two Muslims that night was undeniable. Needless to say, it was a long drive home as I grilled Charlie about what had happened. His answer was on repeat—*God had given him a vision.*

I shared this story with JP not long after it occurred, hoping he would have a logical explanation. Not only did he not provide one, he added to the mystery by telling his own story about Charlie and his visions. Then JP, a self-proclaimed devout atheist, recounted his interaction with Charlie to me:

Charlie was sitting at the bar of my dad's restaurant when he turned to a man sitting next to him, a complete stranger, and said, "You're going to be involved in an accident with an old man who is going to die but it won't be your fault." Charlie then told the man he had seen a vision of the accident and the old man's face seemed to be pressed up close to his face. And also stated that there would be a bunch of cracks or lines near the man's face. He repeatedly told this man, "It won't be your fault". A few days later, that man, that customer from my dad's restaurant, returned visibly shaken, and wanted to speak to my dad about Charlie. He told my dad that he had been in an accident that involved an old man who ended up dying.

The man from the restaurant was driving in the left lane as he was approaching an intersection. The light turned green so there was no need to slow down. He couldn't see that an old man was still walking across the road because a semi-truck in the right lane was blocking his view. By the time he saw the old me, it was too late to stop and the old man was struck by the car. His body landed on the hood of the vehicle, with his face hitting the driver side of the windshield. The impact caused the windshield to crack all around where his face had hit the glass. The impact killed the man instantly. When the police and paramedics arrived, they repeatedly told him that it was not his fault but simply an unfortunate accident. I don't know what to say about this story. There has to be a logical explanation, one that doesn't include God.

When JP finished, I questioned the validity of the story, but JP swore by it and, given his atheistic views, it's hard to imagine he'd have any motivation to make up this story. Especially since the story ended the way they always did, with Charlie saying that he knew what was going to happen because God had given him a vision.

What Is Going On Here?

What confused me most about everything I was seeing and hearing about Charlie's powers was that these visions only seemed to manifest themselves when he was either drunk or high. It made absolutely no sense. Why would God reward him with those amazing powers when he was intoxicated? There were several events like this that I personally witnessed, too many to recount. And there was even a time that both JP and I were present when Charlie was having one of his visions. It was late one night and the three of us were at Denny's (where else?) after a night of drinking. We were sitting in a booth and, as our conversation carried on, an older woman sitting across from us looked in our direction and made eye contact with me. I thought she was being nosy, so I rudely asked her what she was looking at. Before she could respond, Charlie blurted out,

"Your son, Michael, don't worry about his surgery. He's going to be fine."

The lady smiled. "Oh, you know my son Michael?"

"No, but Jesus wanted me to share that with you so that you'd have peace knowing everything would be alright."

The lady's face lit up with shock and she proceeded to tell us about her son and the surgery he was getting ready to have. When she finished speaking, Charlie continued.

"The man you're sitting with is a good man. He's teaching you about God. You should listen to what he says."

When he said that, the man sitting with that woman, whose back had been facing us the entire time, turned his body around and stared at us in disbelief. He told us that they had just met and that he had been teaching her about the Bible. After a few minutes of back and forth, the couple left the restaurant, and JP and I were left speechless. To make things even more bizarre, two younger girls who were sitting in a nearby booth began to engage us in conversation as they had also witnessed what had transpired between Charlie and the couple. During the discussion with those girls, one of them made a comment that she also had the same gift that Charlie had and then she looked at me and said, "One day you're going to write a book for God and it will help people get saved."

Write a book?

CHAPTER 7

The Prostitute and the Atheist

I had just reached the bottom of the stairs heading out the front door when the unfamiliar voice called out: "You're the new guy from upstairs, right?"

I turned to find an older woman at the end of the hallway holding an overflowing laundry basket.

"Yup. Moved in not too long ago."

"Nice to meet you. I'm Cynthia. I live right there." Slurring her words, she pointed to the apartment across from the laundry room. As she approached, I got a closer look at her unruly hair that looked like it hadn't been brushed, let alone washed in several days, as well as the red blotches that covered her skin. She reeked of cigarettes, and when she spoke, I could smell the alcohol on her breath. Cynthia's disheveled appearance hinted at a rough life and years of not taking caring of herself. Prior to that night, I had only heard stories about her from the two girls who lived in the apartment next to mine. When I had first moved in, they inquired if I had met the prostitute who lived on the first floor. I initially laughed at their comment, assuming they were joking, but they were most definitely not. They went on to describe how they would frequently see her, often very late at night, dressed up and getting into expensive vehicles. According to the girls, it was always a different vehicle and a different man picking her up each time. My encounter with Cynthia in the hallway didn't confirm she was a prostitute, but it also didn't rule out the possibility. But I would get my chance to learn more about Cynthia soon enough.

A few nights later, I found myself sitting at my dining room table writing down my thoughts and feelings toward God. I'm not sure what prompted the decision, but I suppose all the conversations with JP and the unexplained visions from Charlie had something to do with it. That or maybe because God still hadn't answered any of my prayers and the frustration I felt over him ignoring me was building to a level that could no longer be kept in. Either way, I decided that this time I would express my words on paper instead.

My bitterness towards God and his continued silence had grown to the level that I no longer had any fear of Him nor did I respect Him. And his loyal subjects, those Christian folks, they annoyed the hell out of me with how brainwashed they seemed to be. They lived robotic lives and, in absence of facts or a legitimate response, they answered everything with some version of needing to have "faith". They believed in a God who had rules that essentially let Him off the hook on a regular basis. When something good happened, they quickly pointed to it being a blessing from God. When something bad occurred, they'd say "It's God's will" or something even more ridiculous like "God works in mysterious ways". And when a prayer didn't get answered, the default response was always "God will answer in his own time". That ideology seemed silly, pure foolishness! Every Christian I had met, including Charlie, seemed like an uneducated, gullible human who never held God accountable to a single thing. And that night, I let God know that I wasn't interested in adhering to a life that required so much out of me, but yet required absolutely nothing out of Him.

The Prostitute & the Virgin

As I poured out my heart and my frustrations on the pages of my notebook, my writing was interrupted by a knock at the front door. The sound startled me, given that it was late and I wasn't expecting any visitors. I made my way to the front door, paused briefly, and returned back to the table to flip over the notebook I had been writing in. I didn't want anyone reading what I had written about God—you know, just in case. I made my way back to the door and looked through the peephole. It was my neighbor Cynthia standing there, wearing a blue dress. My mind immediately drifted to the possibility that Cynthia was a prostitute. If I'm honest, I did wonder if maybe she was coming up to see if I was interested in her *services*. Why else would she show up at my door, unannounced and uninvited, so late at night?

I stood there for a few seconds debating whether I should open up. She knocked again, this time a little more forcefully. I reluctantly opened the door, but before I even had a chance to say a word, she invited herself in, walking right past me towards the family room. I closed the door, taken aback by her aggressiveness.

"How are you?" she asked very sweetly.

How do you respond to that question when a prostitute has forced herself into your apartment at 10:30 at night? I stood there, puzzled. Unsure of where the conversation was going, and skeptical of her motives, I kept my response short, trying to decipher what was going on.

"I'm good, thanks. You?"

"I'm good. Can I sit down?"

I followed again with a short response, "I guess."

She sat down on my couch and proceeded to explain the reason for her visit. "I was heading out for the night and when I got into my car, Jesus told me to come talk to you."

"Jesus? Oh, really?" Unable to hold in my laughter, my retort was cynical and sarcastic. "What did *the Good Lord* want you to tell me?"

She continued, "Well, I was heading out for the night. Actually, I was already in my car, and right before I started it, Jesus told me that I needed to talk to the kid upstairs. That I needed to talk to *you*." I started egging her on, being increasingly antagonistic. Thinking the motive behind her visit was sex, not God, I suggested an alternate possibility.

"Maybe God didn't really tell you that and maybe you just wanted to come up here for some company."

She ignored my snarky comment. "No, He definitely told me to come see you. You don't think He hears you, but He does but you're so mad at Him right now."

The B.S. sirens were going off in my head as I stood there looking down at her as she sat on my couch.

"You're in such a dark place. You're so mad at God that you can't see that He's here with you. It's okay, He's okay that you're mad at Him. He still loves you."

She got up from the couch and began staring at ceiling. She stretched her hands outward and continued looking all around, almost as if she was trying to touch something in the air. She did this for a few seconds while slowly taking several steps away from the couch. "Wow, can you see them? They're all around."

I took a somewhat uncertain posture and hesitantly looked up. "See what?"

"The angels and demons—they're all over," she said as she pointed to the ceiling.

I looked up again, to nothing but a white ceiling, and then directed my confusion toward her.

"It's a battle for your soul. You opened the door to the Devil when you started to doubt God's love for you. But don't worry; you're too important to God and He won't let the Devil steal your soul. But you're going to go through a whole lot, kid. It's going to be hard, but God's going to use it for good and use you for big things for His kingdom. But, you'll have to go through some rough things. Yeah, there is definitely spiritual warfare going on all over this place."

Angels? Demons? War? Pointing towards the door, I forcefully stated, "I think it's time for you to leave."

She calmly rejected my request. "No, no, no. I'm not finished yet." Instead of leaving, Cynthia chose to explore my apartment. By the time I realized what was happening, I found her standing in my bedroom, positioned near the edge of my bed. Yes, a prostitute was in my bedroom! And when she noticed me enter the room, she gave me a little smirk. "Right there." She kneeled near the edge of my bed and tapped the carpet repeatedly. "Here, right here. This is where you kneel and wonder if He hears you. This is where you desperately pray for God to answer you. This is the exact spot where you wonder if God loves you." She got up from the floor and walked past me back out to the family room.

In utter confusion I let Cynthia know that, while I appreciated her comments, I didn't believe that angels or demons were floating around my apartment, and that I didn't believe God spoke to people.

"I know you don't believe it; that's why I'm here tonight. I know you don't believe that I'm telling you the truth, but I am. And I know you don't believe that God cares for you, but He does. God recently sent you someone from your past, an old friend, who talked to you about God, and you didn't believe him either. And you're not going to believe anything I've said tonight. But wait 'til God sends you *the third person*. That's when everything will make sense."

Hide & Seek

Cynthia exited my apartment with no goodbye, walking out just as oddly and quickly as she had entered. I was all alone now and in a state of confusion about all that had transpired. I quickly dismissed Cynthia and the entire night, thinking it would be comical that God would use Cynthia, an alcoholic white trash prostitute, to be his representative. I locked the door and just before shutting off the lights, I noticed the notebook I had been writing in earlier lying on the table. I turned it over and began to read what I had penned, starting with the title: *"Where Are You?"* Cynthia showing up was just a *coincidence*, nothing more, nothing less. I sat down and decided to finish my thoughts on God:

Where Are You?
I've been taught that you are everything
You hear all, you see all, and you know all
And you're there to guide me when I'm lost
They say you have a plan for everyone
And that I'm here for a reason
And all I have to do is believe in you
You forgive me when I do wrong
But desire for me to do right
When I feel weak you are there to give me strength
And when I am strong I should help the weak
But how do I get there?
You haven't given me directions
Except that I need to have faith
But what if I lose that faith?
Will you still love me?
Will you still protect me when my life crumbles?
Are you protecting me now?
I'm sorry but I'm losing faith with every passing day
I'm finding it harder and harder to believe in you
You see it, I know you do
You know how much I struggle everyday
I'm so lost and I thought that you would help
You haven't given me a sign
At least not one that makes sense
I know, be patient, right?
But I'm tired of waiting on you

You say you love me
But where are you?
I don't see you
I can't feel you
I can't hear you
And I've tried
I've tried so hard
I've tried for so long
I used to believe that I was under your shield
And that nothing could harm me
But now, look at me and what I have become
I'm struggling to make sense of all of this
I call to you, I cry to you, I pray to you
I ask you for the simplest things
And my prayers fall on deaf ears, time and time again
So much for your promise to always love me
You'll never leave me?
You'll never forsake me?
Nothing but broken promises
You gave up on me
Why?
Did I not try to do right?
Did I not try to be as good as I knew how to be?
Was I not there for others when they needed me?
I know I did my part
I followed the rules, I did my best and it wasn't enough for you
I wasn't enough for you
I once heard that all I needed to do was call on your name
And you would be there, you would protect me
You would hold me in your arms and tell me you love me
And if I couldn't walk, you would carry me
So tell me where did I go wrong?
What did I do that made you stop loving me?
I'm so confused

Chasing Love   103

I'm alone and I cry every night
I feel my world is crumbling before my very eyes
I can't seem to find happiness in anything I do
No matter how hard I try
I feel like I've been cursed
I lay in silence at night
I look to the heavens
And I ask for a sign
I ask you to tell me you love me
All I ever wanted was for you to say you loved me
But now, who am I supposed to turn to?
The darkness has overcome me
I can't take it anymore
Please hear what I'm saying
Listen to these last words
I'm lost
I'm lonely
I have no strength
I'm hurting
I'm crying
If you ever loved me then please help me
Don't turn your back on me
Don't leave me here all alone
Please don't do this to me
I'm weak and I desperately need your help
I'm on my knees
Please help me
Please
God, where are you?

    I sat there at the table, looking down at the words I had written, and a thought dawned on me. Why was I still calling out to God? Why was I wasting my time pleading with someone who clearly didn't care about me? I took a few minutes to reflect again on the events of the evening. It was an admittedly bizarre night but nothing in me believed that God had orchestrated *any* of it. There was absolutely nothing supernatural about Cynthia acting like a fool or her hope of convincing me that not only had God sent her my way, but that He hears my prayers and that He loves me...and that He was going to *use me for big things*. And truthfully, I couldn't get past the idea that God would use a person *like Cynthia*.

I was a far better person than Cynthia and yet I had never experienced God the way this woman was claiming she did. And if He had actually used her, clearly it meant He does exist and does talk and yet He was choosing to ignore me. In my mind, I couldn't let go of the reality that it seemed like God cared about a lot of people, except *me*, and that was infuriating! I wanted...I needed God to show up, but not by proxy, and if Cynthia was the best representative He could find, I was confident I didn't fit in the world of Christianity. That was when something inside me drastically changed. Something had broken, and I felt it.

Up until that moment, I had only sarcastically considered the possibility that God didn't exist, but with unusual clarity, I realized that I no longer wanted to believe in God. Nothing I had done had worked to usher God's involvement in my life and that was a painful pill to swallow. I concluded it was time to abandon my childish thinking of a supreme celestial being living high above the clouds. I sat there taking inventory of my life and came to the only logical conclusion there was: I had never experienced any benefits of having God in my life. If anything, believing in God had actually caused me more harm than good.

I had been living my life constantly worrying so much for other people, trying to help my parents, that I had lost sight of my health, my needs, my *life*. The weight of all God's rules was crushing me and I was exhausted trying to be a "good person". And besides, nobody around me seemed to be playing by God's rules anyway, and they all seemed happy and successful. Sitting there, I couldn't come up with a single reason to continue believing in God. It was time for a change, a significant one. So I shut off the lights and went to bed, leaving the notebook and my faith behind.

CHAPTER 8

High and Low

Not long after Cynthia's late-night visit and storytelling of angels and demons, she disappeared. She moved out and, to my knowledge, didn't say goodbye to a single person in the unit. All we knew was that one day she was there and the next she was gone. I certainly didn't shed a tear or feel disappointed in any way, because her departure only assured me of no additional late-night visits from a prostitute to discuss God or other imaginary spirits floating around my apartment.

It was at this time that the popularity train that I had been riding for a little more than five years was nearly out of steam. Years of regularly working 12-hour days at the golf course followed by wild all-nighters in the party scene, with little to no sleep, had pushed me to the point of total exhaustion. I was out of energy and no longer had the strength to keep things going. I soon found myself withdrawing from the nightlife more and more, finding excuses not to go out until, eventually, I began avoiding my friends' phone calls altogether. As much as I loved them, the crazy nights no longer brought the same joy they once had. In addition, there had been a steady increase of fighting within the group which had fractured how close we all had once been. Constant arguments turned into gossiping which led to lying, which eventually led to several acts of betrayal. I had been on both ends of the betrayals and after everything had been exposed, the hurt was too much to bear and I quietly removed myself from the group. It had been a long five years; and in that time, I had experienced everything I could have ever imagined and yet it still wasn't enough. The noticeable withdrawal from social activities was an ominous sign that I had entered into a dark new season.

By the fall of 2002, I found myself mostly alone. I was rarely going out with friends, and the relationship with my parents had deteriorated to the point where they hardly ever called to check on me and their visits were few and far between. I wasn't terribly upset by this because that was the whole point of moving out - to reduce the stress of dealing with them - but moving out didn't completely eradicate the carryover of their addictions into my life. My youngest sister was still living at home, and when she called she would inevitably end up talking about my parents and about how things were getting worse at home. It didn't matter where I was, what I was doing or how good of a mood I was in—tension would build up in my head and chest anytime she would talk about my parents. She was the only sibling living at home and I feared the chaos was doing more damage to her than she realized, especially financially. Running out of options, my mom was constantly asking her for money and for a while, my sister would give it to her. She eventually stopped being an ATM to our mother and when that happened, guess whose phone started seeing more frequent calls from Mom?

Being that I was on my own for the first time, it would have been so helpful if those calls would have been to check in on me, but they weren't. Mom's calls were a calculated move. She would disguise the *real* reason she would call by pretending to check on me—asking if I was eating enough or if I was doing well. But the conversation would always change directions and eventually she would ask if I had extra cash lying around, which I never did. I was broke. I had emptied out my savings account to pay for everything in my apartment, from furniture to towels to pots and pans. I was barely surviving, often using my credit cards to pay for food, gas and other essentials. And yet, Mom regularly found ways to make me feel guilty if I didn't give her money, as if I was somehow a terrible son not willing to help his mother! When I'd question why she needed money, there was always an elaborate story that included some "unforeseen event" that had occurred or she was just "a little short" that week. But she was lying. I knew it and she knew it. She wanted money for her gambling addiction. And with no extra cash available, I idiotically began taking cash advances on my credit cards to feed her addiction. Hundreds of dollars each time. The fees for cash advances were high, but the interest rates for not paying them off were even worse. It wasn't long before I found myself thousands of dollars in credit card debt which forced me to begin taking money from one credit card to pay off the minimum for another credit card.

For the first time in my life, money became an issue. Since the time I began working at the golf course when I was 14, I always had money. It was never a lot, but it was enough to cover my expenses—my *own*, anyway! That included my lavish social life of clubs, bars, and the expensive clothes and nice cars that I owned. Now, though, the math simply wasn't adding up and I was constantly finding myself charging most of my monthly expenses with no clue how to pay off the balances. Between the costs associated with living on my own and the constant need to pull money from my credit cards, the debt mounted quickly, and the pressures grew. I felt trapped—unable to afford to live on my own but not willing to move back home and into the hell I had escaped from. Needing an outlet for all the stress, I began to increase my alcohol consumption, not because of a naïve belief that I'd find answers there, but simply because being drunk helped me forget about the problems I had. I suddenly found myself following in the footsteps of my dad.

Things Are Getting Cloudy

At first, drinking worked, and all it took was a few beers each night. But my tolerance for alcohol quickly increased, and a few bottles no longer cut it. I was now regularly spending every night alone on the couch needing to drink a six pack to even remotely feel some relief. And then it grew to eight beers. Then ten. What began as a quick fix now became a lot of work. The effort to get drunk started feeling tiresome so I looked for a quicker method to numb the pain. And there was one, one that I had managed to avoid my entire life. One that had been offered to me dozens and dozens of times. One that I ridiculed my friends for using on a regular basis. Finally, one night, desperate and alone, I grabbed my phone and searched through the contact list until I landed on the one name I knew I could count on: Jimmy. My heart pounded as I anxiously waited for him to answer that call.

"Hello."

"Hey, what are you up to?"

"Working, you?"

"At home. Any chance you want to come over...and well, smoke weed with me?" That's right, I had succumbed to the temptation of something I had avoided my entire life.

Jimmy's voice cracked as he responded, clearly caught off guard. "Really? Now? After all this time?"

"Yeah. You always said that if I ever decided to smoke, you wanted to be the first person to get me high so...here's your chance."

"Seriously, man? You didn't touch weed all these years and now you wanna smoke? You're like 23. If I come over I'm going to get you high. Don't waste my time."

"I won't. I promise."

"Ok, I'm at work. I'll call you when I leave."

"Deal."

Jimmy was once my best friend. From the time we became friends in high school (I was a senior and he was a freshman), we had been inseparable. Growing up with three older sisters, I had always wished for a little brother and Jimmy became mine. Our friendship developed and strengthened over trips to and from school, the mall and dancing the night away at the teenage clubs he and I spent every Friday and Saturday night at. He and I were closer to each other than anyone else in the group. We did everything together and had our own world of inside jokes, which bothered the rest of the friends in our group. But over time, as our circle of friends got bigger and the craziness of our partying increased, the closeness Jimmy and I had once shared started to fracture. When weed entered into the picture, Jimmy took hold of it more than anyone else. Weed became such a big part of his life that it dramatically changed him. He was no longer the best friend I had known and loved. He became unreliable and all the lies he told eroded all the trust I had in him. Our friendship had deteriorated so badly that the tension exploded one night, resulting in a fist fight in my parents' driveway in front of several of our friends. After the dust had settled, we tried to repair the damage on several occasions. But all the lies, betrayals and hurts were too difficult to forget and, ultimately, our friendship was never the same.

Jimmy and I hadn't hung out in a while. I don't think either of us envisioned the first time he was going to get me high would be at age 23 and at a time when he and I were barely speaking, but that's how things went. Surprisingly, Jimmy didn't come alone. He brought along a female coworker of his, which made the evening a little more awkward for everyone. After a little bit of catching up, we finally got around to the whole purpose of the night—smoking weed. Jimmy pulled out a tightly wrapped blunt from his coat pocket and proceeded to light it up. The leather couch made that familiar crunching sound as he laid back and exhaled a heavy cloud of smoke. He took another long puff and then attempted to pass the blunt my way. I declined and encouraged his friend to go next. He and I both knew I was just stalling but he passed it anyway and after she took a few puffs, all eyes were on me. It was time. I had stalled long enough.

After taking a puff, I handed the blunt back to Jimmy to no avail. Jimmy pushed it back and commented that I hadn't even inhaled yet. I tried again but was still unable to inhale correctly. Seeing my struggles, Jimmy took the blunt back and asked me to cup my hands around my lips, open my mouth wide and inhale as deep as I could. So I complied and before I realized what was going on, Jimmy was blowing smoke through the blunt and toward my cupped hands. I began coughing uncontrollably, choking in the process. I jumped off the couch and ran toward the kitchen. Bent over the sink, gasping for air, I tried to pour water down my throat to stop the coughing. After the coughing subsided, I headed back to the couch feeling a little woozy and quite embarrassed. Jimmy and his friend sat on the couch laughing, clearly enjoying my inexperience.

"How you feeling?"

"I'm not sure. My throat is killing me. It's burning. And my heart is racing."

"Give it a few minutes, you'll be fine."

I felt lightheaded and there was a tingling sensation in my hands, arms and face. Jimmy assured me those were all normal effects and nothing to worry about. And then the high began. Unlike the night of trying ecstasy where the high gave me tons of energy – after the 20 minutes of hell – being high from weed had the complete opposite effect. I had no energy whatsoever, but

I also didn't have a care in the world. I found it hard to even think as my entire body went numb. This was exactly what I had been looking for—a way to quickly numb myself, and weed did exactly that. There was a period of silence as we all enjoyed our individual high. Jimmy and his friend continued smoking the blunt while I remained locked in my own world—sitting silently and showing indifference to their presence. Shortly after, the two got up to leave but not before providing me with two joints as *"gifts"* for later. I sat there alone in my apartment focusing on the tingling in my body and the numbness I felt in my head. I didn't have a care in the world. I had finally found a way to forget about all of life's problems. Everything inside my mind disappeared and, for the first time in a long time, the pain was gone and the chaos of life seemed miles away. I now knew how to quiet the voices in my head and erase the sorrow in my heart with very little effort. I laid on my couch the rest of the evening looking at the flame flickering from the candle on the coffee table. Music played softly in the background as I drifted away. *I was finally free.*

How to Escape Life

A couple of days later, I was sitting half-asleep during an early morning class and all I could think about was getting high. Instead of being a responsible college student, I decided to ditch my remaining classes so I could go home and smoke weed. I walked into my apartment, grabbed one of the joints Jimmy had left that were still on the coffee table and headed to the bedroom. I put on some music, laid on the bed and lit up the joint. I still didn't know how to inhale properly but I managed to figure it out. The clock hadn't even hit noon and there I was, getting high in my bedroom instead of being in class. There was definitely a feeling of guilt about the whole thing but that quickly vanished as the high began and the numbness I was craving for returned. The next day, I decided to get high before I went to class so that I wouldn't spend the day at school thinking about it. But by the time I arrived at school, I was so high and feeling paranoid to be around people that I immediately turned around and drove back home—ditching another day of classes. Once home, I smoked again, finishing off what was left of the second joint before passing out on the couch. I woke up later that afternoon wanting to smoke again but I was out of drugs. I didn't want to call Jimmy to buy drugs out of concern for what he might think about me and I didn't trust that he wouldn't share this information with the other guys in our group of friends. So instead I reached out to a coworker and later that day he came over. Not only did we smoke, but I purchased my first eighth of weed from him. After that, I began calling him regularly to come over to smoke and sell me drugs.

I soon developed a routine—going to work or school, coming home, getting high and falling asleep. Those first few months of drug use were spent doing a lot of sleeping, until my body learned how to function while being high. I went from smoking half a joint to a full joint in one sitting. Then onward I went to smoking two joints, and then I graduated to smoking blunts, which soon got bigger and bigger. I just wanted to be high. It was all I could think about and it was the only thing that allowed me to function. As my drug use increased, so did the cost to get high, and already heavily in debt, I began selling weed to some of my friends to offset the cost of my own addiction. That's right, I became a dope dealer.

Spring of 2003 arrived, and my apartment lease was up. I couldn't afford to keep living on my own so I had a decision to make: do I return home or do I continue living on my own, getting further and further into debt? Continued debt still had more appeal than trying to salvage the relationship I had with my parents. So instead of moving back home, I sought out a cheaper apartment in a less desirable area. A few days after moving into my new place, I noticed that the hallway reeked of weed. I initially thought the smell was coming from my apartment and that I needed to do a better job containing the odor. But it turned out that the smell wasn't coming from my apartment at all—well, not entirely. Almost everyone in the complex smoked weed. As luck would have it, the guy living in the apartment underneath mine was a dealer. Access to weed became unbelievably easy and I no longer needed to bother my friend from work. Getting drugs was as simple as a 10-step walk down the staircase.

Not only did getting drugs become extremely easy, my neighbor was selling some pretty amazing stuff. It was a lot more potent than what was going around at that time and when word got around, the amount of friends who wanted to buy weed from me increased significantly. I was soon getting calls from several people every Friday night wanting to spend part of their paycheck on the drugs I was selling. As I increased the amount of weed I was selling, I began smoking even more. I had no sober moments in my new apartment. I was high 24/7 and the drug use was starting to show on my body. I had lost a lot of weight, I looked thin in the face, and my eyes were often bloodshot and darkly ringed.

That summer marked my 10th year working at the golf course and my sixth as an Assistant Manager under Jeff. Over the years, he had entrusted me with more and more responsibilities, and I became his go-to assistant. I devoted my life to that golf course and it was the only thing I could depend on. The members had watched me grow up before their eyes and most, if not all, saw me as this responsible young man. They were certainly unaware of all the chaos in my personal life, and how would they have known? I had mastered the ability to conceal truth and had shoved all the pain and hurt so far inside that all they saw was a polite, clean-shaven employee day after day, month after month and year after year. Heck, I never even showed up late, not once, and I never had even a hint of alcohol on me, even on mornings I walked into work after an entire night of partying. I had arrogantly thought I was hiding my personal struggles so well, fooling the members all along the way. So it came as a heart-dropping moment one morning when Jeff pulled me into his office to "talk".

What Goes Up Must Come Down

He shut the door of his office, sat in his leather chair and asked me to sit in the chair across from him. He voiced his concerns about my physical appearance and mentioned that I looked tired, that I had lost weight, and that joy I used to have no longer existed. He was absolutely right, but it was hard to hear those words because nobody, including my family, had even noticed. What made things a lot more emotional was that his concerns were shared by several members at the golf course, specifically the women. He informed me that several of them that I had gotten to know well over the years had approached him privately to ask if I was alright. They had offered concern over my physical appearance and were voicing such worries out of genuine motherly love. I sat there across from Jeff and absolutely broke down in front of him. To think that my boss and these women at work were so concerned about my health, and yet somehow my own family couldn't see it? Did my parents just not care or were they just so lost in their own addictions, their own pain, and their own misery, that they couldn't see mine? Clearly the signs of my own addiction were there, and I resented my parents for not seeing it. But they were addicts as well. It never dawned on me at the time that it would have been virtually impossible for them to look past their own problems to notice what was happening to me.

I was too embarrassed to tell Jeff anything more than what he knew, which was everything except the drug use. I left out the gory details of how heavily addicted I had become to drugs, how I had become a drug dealer and how I was constantly high…including during that very conversation we were having. I lied to him and blamed the stress of my parents as the reason for my unhealthy appearance. My relationship with Jeff was the most important one I had at that time. I had worked for him going on 10 years and he was the only reliable person I knew. He was straightforward with his expectations and I loved that. I didn't have to wonder with him – I knew exactly where I stood. And throughout the years, especially during the winter seasons when the golf course was closed, Jeff and I worked closely in the basement fixing up the golf carts. Jeff taught me everything I knew about how to repair golf carts and doing general maintenance types of things, the way I suppose most dads teach their sons as they grow up. But I didn't grow up sharing moments like that with my dad so the time alone with Jeff was very special to me. I loved him like a father.

We'd have long conversations about the issues I was dealing with at home with my parents and he knew the horror stories intimately. He knew about my mom's gambling addiction and my dad's drinking problem. He knew about the physical abuse I witnessed on an almost nightly basis. He knew why I moved out and why I was financially strapped. He knew the stress it was causing and the anger I was holding inside. And when I was arrested for fighting with my dad at age 18, he invited me to come live with him and his family. I still regret my decision to turn down his offer but at the time, I was young and afraid to walk away from my family. But I'll never forget the love and compassion he showed me that day.

As Jeff and I continued our conversation in his office, I didn't fear getting fired. He wouldn't have done that even if I told him about the drugs I sold or about the addiction I had. But what I did fear was him knowing just how far I had fallen. I was ashamed of what I had become. I feared disappointing him and having him see me differently. I didn't want to lose being known as his most reliable and hardest working assistant. I was afraid to lose what had taken me 10 years to build. And in my heart, I knew he would have done everything he could to get me help, but I was afraid to face the reality that my life was a complete mess. So I did what I had become really good at doing – I hid the truth and convinced him I was happy and that he had nothing to worry about.

No Good Deed Goes Unpunished

Life kept coming at me hard and added pressure came a few weeks later when I learned that my mom had filed for bankruptcy. Her credit cards were taken away and, in addition, she began having her paycheck garnished. Part of me was happy that she had hit rock bottom; but, at the same time, I hurt for her. She had made a mess of her life and it broke my heart to hear her say that she didn't even have a few extra dollars in her purse or that she could barely pay for gas or food. As angry as I was towards her, she was still my mom and I loved her, and I couldn't just stand by and watch her suffer like that. Not knowing what else to do, I called up one of my credit card companies and added my mom as an authorized user. A week later a new credit card with her name on it arrived in the mailbox. I immediately called Mom and invited her out to lunch. We met at Applebee's and it was the first time I had seen her in a long while. From the moment I saw her, I could see the distress written all over her face. I couldn't help but wonder if she paid the same attention to what had become of my appearance. I opened up the conversation sharing with my mom that I wanted us to have a better relationship. After that, I began to explain the real reason for our lunch date. "Mom, I know it must be tough to be without money and without a credit card." I reached in my pocket and I pulled out the Discover card with her name on it and slid it across the table.

She looked down at the card, shocked. "Why are you doing this?"

"Mom, what if you're stranded somewhere? What if there's an emergency? What if you need food or gas?"

She began crying at the table and agreed to take the card but assured me she would only use it for emergencies.

"Please, Mom, don't screw me over. I would never be able to forgive you if you hurt me with this."

"I'm your mother. I would *never* do that to you."

Even though she had brought this all upon herself with her own gambling addictions, I couldn't watch my mom struggle to pay for basic needs like food and gas. And I was trying to repair our strained relationship by doing anything I could to help her, even with all the insurmountable wreckage going on in my own life. I knew it was a risky move to give her access to my credit card, but I wanted to believe it was going to mend our relationship and I wanted to believe that a mother would not purposely hurt her child's financial situation. Those are the kinds of poor decisions a person makes when they are driven by emotion instead of logic.

A month later, Mom called me. "Hey, I want to come over and see you. Are you free?"

"Yeah, sure. Come over and I'll make us dinner."

An hour later she walked into my apartment and hugged and kissed me, but she didn't go past the family room. She stood there watching me make food and then there was complete silence. I looked up from the food I was stirring and noticed her slumped over near the table. She lowered her head. "I did something really bad."

I stared at her with a sour feeling in my stomach. I knew what was coming. I knew exactly what the next words out of her mouth were going to be.

"I used your credit card at the casino." She began crying and fell to the floor, curled up against the wall like a baby. My anger got the best of me and I threw the dish on the floor, shattering it into hundreds of pieces. I then took the other dish from the table, one filled with the dinner I had made for her and also threw that on the floor. I screamed at her for several minutes, berating her like a child.

"You promised me! You swore you wouldn't screw me over! I told you I would never forgive you if you did this to me." I didn't let her talk and resorted to kicking my own mother out of my apartment.

How could she do this to me? How could she betray me like this? I was once again being punished for doing a good thing and hurt fueled my anger as I looked for an outlet to unleash my fury. Then I saw it – the cross on the wall, a gift my sister had bought for me while on vacation in Cancun. I grabbed it off the wall and snapped it in half. I went into my bedroom and found the bible buried deep in my closet and began ripping the pages out of it. *"Fuck you,* God! I hate you, I fucking hate you! You are nowhere to be found. I can't believe that I was a good person, and I tried to help, and this is how I get repaid. I can't believe she betrayed me! And you allowed it!"

After that night, it made no sense to try anymore. I hated my life and everyone around me. I couldn't take it anymore and a desire for revenge, especially toward my mom, burned like wildfire within me. My mind went dark and over the next several months, I became fixated on suicide as my only way out. Every night ended with me sitting on the floor locked in my bathroom smoking weed for hours contemplating how and when to kill myself.

My world had closed in on me and I felt trapped. I continued sinking deeper and deeper, drowning in an ocean of despair. The light turned dim and it got harder and harder to see any hope. Falling seemed easier than trying to face the daunting task of climbing out of the hell my life had become. And then there was that mirror in the bathroom. That fucking mirror with the same damn reflection looking back at me. I hated that reflection! It was high school all over again. Only this time, there was nothing to pray for to make the problem go away. When I stood in front of that high school mirror crying as I ate lunch, I at least had hope as I prayed to "God" to come and rescue me. But now there was nothing. There was no hope left. There was no one coming to rescue me. There was no one to help me. There was no God.

CHAPTER 9

Hit by a Boulder

I t had been almost two years since I moved out of my parents' home and, in that time, everything in life had changed for the worse. I had become a full-blown drug addict, needing to get high just to function during the day and needing even more drugs just to fall asleep at night. I had quit working at the golf course after 10 years and had dropped out of college. I went from having money in the bank and the ability to buy almost anything I wanted to suddenly finding myself nearly $40,000 in credit card debt. And that debt didn't even include an additional $15,000 I owed in student loans for a college degree I never finished.

The years of clubbing and partying were a distant memory – as I exchanged my wild social life for quiet nights in my apartment sitting alone by candlelight getting high. I had pushed away what remained of my friends out of fear they would realize just how bad my addiction had become and replaced them with the guys I had worked with at the golf course. Up until that last year, I had never spent time with any of them socially. But now the drugs bonded us and they became my new circle of friends. We were hanging out regularly, which really only meant that we were getting high together. They were younger than me and still living with their parents, so they would come over to my apartment to smoke a few joints. But while it was fun, I couldn't wait until they left. Not because I didn't like them but rather because, when they left, that was when my real drug use began.

I smoked with these new friends to have fun; I smoked by myself to forget. And when they'd leave, I'd be right back in the bathroom on the floor smoking until I could barely move. After my body and mind were completely numb, I would pull myself off the floor and stare at the drug addict in the mirror for long periods of time wondering what had happened to me. My mind would drift back to the days in high school as a lonely teenager staring in that bathroom mirror, eating his lunch. That boy had gotten everything he wished for – he became unbelievably popular beyond anything he could have ever imagined. He had experienced so much in such a short period of time, more than most people probably do in their lifetime. Yet it didn't fix a damn thing. In the end, that boy ended up right back in front of a mirror, alone and ashamed. My life had truly come full circle.

The downward spiral I was in seemed insurmountable. I was on a collision course with my very own black hole hell, a place completely absent of light or hope. With no way to escape, I fell a little further each day and ended each night hugging my pillow as I cried myself to sleep. My mind was tormented and the hurt inside was real. The freedom I thought I had bought when I moved out wasn't freedom at all. Nothing had worked out the way I had hoped it would and I found myself resigned to the inevitable. With no hope left, suicide was the only way out of the hell I was in. And it was time.

April 17, 2004. As the calendar inched closer to the 21st, memories of that fateful day – when my world collapsed, began to resurface. It had been nearly two years, yet I still couldn't shake the regret of losing Amanda. I attempted to clear my head with drugs and a long drive, but found no solace so I turned my car around and headed home. But not before I made a quick stop at the liquor store across the street from my apartment to pick up blunt wraps. While inside paying the cashier, I heard a voice say, "You look like that guy from Linkin Park." I lifted my head and looked toward the direction the voice had come from. At the far end of the store was a light-brown haired middle-aged woman leaning against the counter. She smiled and repeated herself, "You look like the guy from Linkin Park."

"Are you talking to me?"

"Yeah."

"Are you referring to Linkin Park, as in the music group?"

"Yeah, you look like that one guy."

I didn't agree with her comparison but wanted to be cordial, so I nodded my head and returned the smile. I completed the transaction with the cashier, grabbed the blunt wraps, and nodded again at the woman as I walked past her and out of the store.

Sleepwalking at Midnight

April 20. I returned home from work, ate dinner, rolled up a large blunt, and began smoking for several hours before eventually passing out on the couch. When I woke up later that evening, the candle I had lit earlier was nearly melted to its core, dripping all over the coffee table in the middle of the room. Groggy and disoriented, I stumbled toward the bedroom but felt agitated as I struggled to get comfortable in bed. Suddenly and seemingly out of nowhere, I heard a voice. Although it was gentle, almost whisper-like, it was distinct and it said to go across the street to the liquor store. I initially ignored the voice thinking it was simply a thought in my head. But as I continued to toss and turn, I heard the voice a second time and it repeated itself:

"Go across the street to the liquor store."

This time I sat up in bed because the voice was clearly not in my head. It was real. But I had smoked a lot of weed, so I once again dismissed the voice thinking I was just being paranoid. I laid back down and, just as I had finally gotten comfortable and felt myself beginning to doze off, the voice came back for a third time. Only this time, it was louder and more specific.

"Go to the store across the street. The lady you met the other night is going to be there and she has something important to tell you."

I was now more than paranoid, I was completely freaked out and there was absolutely no chance I was going to fall asleep. So I hopped out of bed and quickly threw on the pair of jeans lying on the floor. I grabbed my grey hoodie and my car keys and headed out of my apartment. A minute later, I was pulling into the parking lot of the liquor store wondering what the hell I was getting myself into. It was late, I was exhausted and high, and I had no business being there. But I walked in and quickly surveyed the store only to find it empty, with the exception of the cashier. I headed toward the back of the store where the coolers were located and grabbed a bottled water. As I made my way toward the front counter, a voice loudly proclaimed,

"Hey, Linkin Park boy. You're here!"

I lifted my head and lowered the hood of my sweater. Standing in front of me was the older woman I had met a few days before.

Smiling, she asked, "Do you remember me from the other night?"

I nodded, "Yeah, I do."

Still smiling, she continued, "I knew you were going to be here tonight."

Her comment startled me.

"How did you know?"

"Well, I was on my way to work when you suddenly popped in my head and I knew I was supposed to come here."

"What do you mean 'you came here'? Don't you work here? You are behind the counter, right?"

"No, I work at OnStar...you know, like for your car. I just come here a lot so I sometimes hang out behind the counter."

"So you were driving to work and I popped in your head?"

"Yea, I was driving, listening to Building 429, which is my favorite Christian band, and a picture of your face popped in my head. God told me I needed to come here tonight because you were going to be here, and that I needed to talk to you."

I remember smirking a little bit thinking it was interesting that her favorite band included the numbers 429 – April 29 is my birthday.

"Okay, so you were driving, listening to music, and God told you to come here to talk to me? What for?"

"I think I'm supposed to talk to you about surrendering your life to Jesus."

"So let me get this straight...God told you that. Sure. I think I'm good with all that. Thanks, though. I don't really believe in God."

Having already been down this road a few times before, I had zero interest in hearing from another Christian, especially since they all sounded like pre-programmed robots saying the exact same thing every time. Besides, nothing good had ever happened by talking to those Jesus freaks.

Seemingly undeterred, the woman ignored my response and began to share a story about how, when she was younger, she aborted a baby boy. She went into detail as she described how the decision had haunted her throughout her adult life and turned her into an addict as she tried to cope with the regret she carried. Continuing, she let me know that she had a serious gambling addiction as well, which she stated caused her to be a terrible mother to her other child. She concluded by telling a third story, one that was a little far-fetched. She claimed to have been in a car accident where an electrical pole fell on her vehicle. The live wires surrounded her car leaving her trapped inside with no way to get out. The paramedics and fire department finally arrived but they were unable to reach her, and she feared she was going to be electrocuted before they could rescue her. While she waited in the vehicle, she claimed an angel appeared in the car to comfort and protect her during the whole ordeal.

That, of course, was a little much for me. An angel sitting shotgun in her vehicle? Not so fast. Wouldn't an angel be powerful enough to move the wires and free her? If an angel is from God, why would the angel still need the electric company to shut off the power? And why would she need the paramedics? She went on to say that she got "saved" that night and became a "born again Christian". There were those words again, "born again". I still had no idea what it meant, but what I did know was that I had encountered too many people who sounded just like her and I wasn't interested in what she was selling. Every time one of these Christian folks popped into my life, things seemed to only get worse. Eager to end the dialogue, I let her know that I was happy for her but that I was not a Christian and was not interested in those types of things.

"I think you should surrender your life to Jesus. Jesus loves you. He knows the things you're going through and He's waiting for you. All you need to do is come to Him. Let Him heal you. Let Him save you." She paused momentarily. "You know, I think God is telling me that you should come with me to church."

I had been polite and had allowed her to tell her stories, even though I knew they were made up. Annoyed with her unwillingness to respect my beliefs, I responded sternly, "I just told you, I don't believe in God and I have no interest in going to church. I want nothing to do with God."

But this lady would not let it go.

"Please, I know you're hurting, but God wants to heal that hurt. I know that God brought us together and I'm just asking that you have a little faith. Please just give me your number. I cannot let you leave without it."

In an effort to end the conversation, I told her I'd consider going to church with her someday. She read way too much into my comment and jumped at the opportunity to hand me a scrap paper from her purse, as well as a pen to jot down my number. It didn't matter one way or the other; I was never going to church with her so I gave her my number with no intentions of ever seeing her again.

The following day I arrived home from work a little after 5 p.m. I began rolling up a blunt, one larger than normal. It was a significant day – April 21, the worst day on the calendar for me. It had now been exactly two years since Amanda had broken my heart, and in those two years, my life had been nothing but hell. I didn't blame her for all my problems, but she seemed to be the catalyst marking the moment where life headed in the downward direction it did. As I finished rolling the blunt, my cell phone rang from an unknown number. I answered it and a woman's voice politely said, "Hello, it's Charlotte." There were a few seconds of silence as I searched my memory for who I knew named Charlotte. Problem was, I didn't know any.

"Who?"

"Charlotte, from last night. The liquor store."

It then dawned on me that during the course of the conversation the previous night, we hadn't exchanged names.

"Oh, hello, Charlotte."

"I'd like to invite you to attend church with me."

"I know, you mentioned that last night. And I told you that I would think about it."

"Well, I want you to go tonight. I think you're supposed to come with me to church. Tonight."

I had never heard of anyone going to church on a Wednesday, and I let her know that I thought the idea was ridiculous and that I was busy.

"Please, I really need you to come to church with me. I really believe God wants to show you something tonight." The idea of going to church on a Sunday was bad enough, but it was a *Wednesday*. I had a miserable day at work...and all I was thinking about was getting high in hopes of forgetting that April 21 existed.

"I'm begging you; you have to come with me to church."

What Did I Get Myself Into?

I don't remember what exactly happened that changed my decision, but after several minutes of her begging and pleading, I was finally persuaded to join her at her church. Perhaps I was tired of her begging. Perhaps I was curious to see what was going to happen. Perhaps...I held on to a sliver of hope that there really was a God, one who hadn't forgotten about me.

Her church was located in Northville, about a twenty-minute drive from where I was living. To make things easier on me, she suggested we meet up at the Speedway gas station near her church and then I would follow her the rest of the way there. After we hung up, I immediately regretted my decision and debated whether or not to even show up. I didn't owe this lady anything and I'd probably never see her again anyway, so who cared if I blew her off? My conscience got the better of me and I decided against flaking but not before I called for backup – my old friend Charlie. Church was his territory and I figured at least I wouldn't feel so out of place if he was there. He agreed to join without needing much convincing. Not long after we spoke, he was knocking on my front door with a duffle bag in his hand.

The plan was for Charlie to spend the night after we came back from church, something he had done often over the years. When he entered my apartment, he put his bag on the glass dining room table while I finished getting ready. But just as we were ready to head out, he pulled a 180 and decided not to go. I stood there frustrated, wondering why the heck he drove all the way to my apartment if he wasn't planning on going. He didn't provide an answer and just picked up his bag from the table and left. I was pissed! But what could I do? I got in my car and headed to the Speedway to meet up with Charlotte. When I arrived, Charlotte was sitting in her white Toyota Camry waiting, just as she told me she would be. She got out of her car and headed toward mine. "The church is down the street. Just follow me."

We arrived at her church a few minutes later and entered a large auditorium where young kids were playing music on the stage. These kids couldn't have been more than high schoolers at best, some looking even younger. There were a decent amount of people standing up clapping and waving their hands in the air to the music. This was not what I had expected whatsoever. It was nothing like the Orthodox Church I had grown up in where folks sat on wooden benches, stood up and sat down on command at the ring of a bell, and crossed themselves a dozen times, all the while remaining virtually silent. In the Orthodox Church, there were absolutely no drum sets – or guitars being played, and there was no clapping or waving of hands in the air either. Charlotte's church seemed more rock concert and less church. I even distinctly remember the song the kids were singing when I entered the room because it had the most ridiculous lyrics: "Every day, it's you I live for. Every day, I follow after you. Every day, I walk with you, my Lord."

I felt stupid for agreeing to all of this and was desperate to leave but didn't know the best way to exit without looking like a complete jerk. By this point, Charlotte was engulfed in the music. Her hands were stretched out as far as they could be toward the ceiling and her eyes were closed. I, on the other hand, had my hands in my pocket as I fumed internally at the lunacy I allowed myself to partake in. After a few more songs had played, Charlotte abruptly looked at me and announced, "I think it's time for us to leave." I was surprised but certainly welcomed her change of heart. We walked out of the church before the music even ended. As we headed toward the parking lot, Charlotte suggested that we find a place to get coffee. "I made a mistake. Maybe this wasn't where I was supposed to take you tonight. But please don't go home. Let's just go somewhere and talk. I really believe there is a reason God wants us together tonight."

I could see in Charlotte's eyes that her plea was authentic. She was a very kind person and I'm sure she had good intentions. And she probably did truly believe that her God had ordained our chance meeting, but my heart was so hardened that I didn't even care if there was a God. I had been a good sport, but I didn't see the value in continuing the night. If Charlotte was really sent by Him, why was the church experience an epic failure? I had given God His chance and yet again He let me down.

Even though my intention was to say no, something inside me seemingly forced me to agree to her request. She didn't know of any nearby coffee houses so she asked that I follow her. We got in our cars and I watched as Charlotte drove past multiple places where coffee was served. I couldn't help but wonder why she was being so picky on the place to drink coffee. Come on, lady, just pick a freaking place already! She finally pulled into an almost empty parking lot, but it wasn't a coffee house she had taken me to. It was a bar called Boulders near downtown Plymouth, just down the street from where I had grown up. We both exited our cars and I kept my comments to myself, not wanting to antagonize her by questioning her motive for taking me to a bar instead of a coffee shop.

Is This Really Happening?

We entered Boulders and with the exception of a few people, the place was mostly empty. If I'm honest, I was a little embarrassed being at a bar with a much older woman, so I suggested we sit in one of the booths lining the windows since they provided a little more privacy and less chance of people looking at us. Charlotte accepted my suggestion but needed to use the restroom first. As I sat there, alone, looking out the window, I thought about how I had driven past this bar thousands of times over the years but had never gone inside. Interestingly, the bar we were in was located right in the heart of downtown Plymouth – a place I had spent so much time hanging out with friends over the years. Downtown Plymouth was also the same location where I had first met Amanda years ago. As my mind began to drift back to better times in my life, a woman's voice interrupted.

"Welcome to Boulders. Can I get you…?"

The voice trailed off without completing the question, so I looked away from the window and to my right, standing before me was Amanda. Yes, *that* Amanda. It was like seeing a ghost. My heart dropped. It was as if all the air was sucked out of the bar. The last time I had spoken to Amanda was just before her wedding when she told me she was moving to Alabama. After that call, I expected to never speak with her again, let alone see her again. But there she was, standing right in front of me, wearing an apron and ready to take my order.

"I figured it was only a matter of time before we ran into each other," she said.

How many sleepless nights spent thinking about what I should have said to her the night she ended things with me? How many speeches had I rehearsed in my head? How many tears shed over the mistake I made with her? And now, I had my chance to say everything I wanted but never got the chance to. I desperately wanted to tell her how badly she had broken my heart. And how alone I was. And how empty my life had been. But none of that came out. I couldn't muster up the courage to confess what had been eating away at me for two long years. And instead, all Amanda got from me was a feeble attempt at small talk.

"I'm confused, weren't you moving to Alabama?"

"We did, but we didn't like it so we moved back to Michigan." She continued talking but her words were muffled. It was as if I were under water, struggling to hear. Struggling to breathe. My eyes were fixed on the diamond ring sparkling on her left hand. I knew she was married but seeing the ring in person, I don't know, it was like a gut punch. My mind was racing all over the place, still in shock that, of all the places I could have ended up tonight, it was here, in this bar, on this night, on this *date*. She had ended things with me exactly two years ago to the day and for two years my life had been hell. The downward spiral began and the floodgates of hell opened up on this very date, April 21, exactly two years ago.

For those two long years, I had wasted countless hours trying to figure out why I still hadn't gotten over Amanda and why I continued to think there was a purpose that she had been in my life in the first place. I had driven myself crazy wondering if I had made a mistake not fighting for her and regretting not trying harder to win her heart. I spent so much time wondering if she was still married, if she was happy, if she still thought about me. And just a couple of hours earlier, I was at home ready to get high to forget this miserable day existed, so how the hell could she now be my waitress?

I don't remember much about the rest of the conversation, except for where Amanda was currently living. It was a city that was roughly 40 minutes away, which only added to the confusion. I'm sure there were bars and restaurants a lot closer to her home that she could have been working at. So again I asked myself, *why was she here?*

Charlotte's return from the bathroom thrusted me back into the reality of the moment. It also added more awkwardness to the table. I'm sure Amanda was wondering why I was at a bar with a much older woman but she stayed the course and asked what we wanted to drink. When Amanda returned with them, she informed us her shift was ending and that another waitress was going to take over. I had harbored so much regret, which fueled so much of my anger toward her over the years. I spent two years hating her for what she had done but seeing her again, my heart let me know that I didn't hate her at all. I just missed her. I missed talking to her. I missed seeing her. I missed everything about her. And now she was leaving me again, like she had done two years prior.

As I watched Amanda turn and walk away, I looked toward Charlotte and told her I was done. Charlotte could tell something had happened, so she didn't put up a fight. I paid for our drinks and we walked out of the bar.

The Long Way Home

That drive home was hell. It's hard to adequately explain the thoughts that were circling around in my head. It wasn't just seeing Amanda again that bothered me; it was all the events that led to seeing her, starting with the first night I saw Charlotte in the liquor store. And the voice that prompted me to go back to speak with her a few nights later. And being coerced to giving her my number and accepting the invitation to attend church. I wondered what would have happened if Charlie hadn't bailed and joined us at church? Or what if Charlotte hadn't abruptly decided to leave church early? If any of those things hadn't happened, I would not have run into Amanda again.

My wrath was aimed straight toward God. Charlotte had stated God was guiding her actions, so what was I to think? Charlotte had been saying how much God cared for me, how much He loved me and had been there for me, but here I was again getting slapped in the face by

God! If He existed, He had once again deliberately gone out of His way to hurt me in the deepest possible way. This wasn't love. This was vengeance.

I should have never run into Amanda again. I wasn't supposed to come face-to-face with the worst decision I had ever made. Why did I even agree to go to the damn church in the first place? And why did God feel it necessary to put me in a situation where all this happened? Why did He hate me so much? Why did He continually do things to hurt me? Why was He so vindictive?

By the time I returned home, the emotion from seeing Amanda, the confusion over Charlotte, and the anger toward God fueled a night of drug use far beyond what I had ever experienced. I sat there on the bathroom floor – with the door shut and a heart that had been shattered into a thousand pieces as I desperately tried to ease the pain. The drug use lasted for hours, engulfing me and the entire bathroom in a thick haze of smoke to the point that it was almost impossible to recognize where I was. And when my brain had become completely fried and my body had become so numb that I couldn't lift my hands let alone get up off the cold bathroom tile, I slouched against the door and felt the darkness of sleep settle in. Before my eyes shut, I offered up one last prayer to God – a desperate plea to never wake up again.

CHAPTER 10

Twenty-second

April 22, 2004. Another day in a world I no longer wanted to be part of. And the plan was to make it my last. The events from the night before had my head spinning without the slightest idea of how to explain what I had witnessed. The day was spent in a fog-like haze as I returned home from work. When I entered my apartment, I could only make it as far as the hallway before falling to the floor, overwhelmed by the desire to end it all. It was as if there was some force out there in the world making sure to keep its foot on my neck, and the constant battle had worn me down. I just couldn't keep fighting it. The heaviness of life had been building for years and it was relentless. I was tired, I had no more energy left and I was broken. I wanted out.

I sat there on the floor, facing the hard reality that I had been on the losing end of every transaction, with almost everyone I had encountered. My life was a mess, a far cry from all the dreams I had while growing up. Facing death was now a more welcomed option than facing the fear of living another day in a world that had provided me nothing but years of heartache, disappointment and loneliness. My spirit was broken and I had nothing left to give. I needed a way out of this life and I wanted it all to end that night. I concluded that a high-speed car crash would be the quickest and easiest way to end my suffering. My plan was to get on the highway and drive as fast as my car would allow, remove the seat belt and crash head-on into any concrete structure I could find. I played the scenario over and over in my mind as I sat on the floor. I rolled one last blunt, for one last high, knowing that it would all soon be over and I would finally have the peace that had eluded me for years. My mind was completely consumed by morbid thoughts of death, what the accident would look like, how mutilated my body would end up and what people would say after I was gone. Would they have regrets for how they treated me? Then, it dawned on me…nobody loved me so would anyone really even *care* that I was dead?

Just then, my cell phone rang. It was Charlotte and she was apologetic from the moment I answered.

"I'm sorry about last night. I'm sorry if I did something wrong. I know you were really upset when we left the bar, and I'm truly sorry for that." There was a genuineness in her words, a loving motherly voice filled with compassion as she spoke. It might have been the first time anyone had truly apologized to me and the irony was that she had nothing to be sorry for. I let her know that my behavior the night before had nothing to do with her and that I just wanted to be alone. She continued, "I'm convinced that God sent me to you. I prayed for you all last night and Jesus spoke clearly to me about you. Jesus wants to save you. He wants to heal your heart. He knows how hurt you are by all that has happened over the past few years. He knows everything you're dealing with. He knows about your mom's gambling addiction and how hard you've tried to help her. He knows about your financial problems and how you were betrayed by your close friends. He knows all of it, and He wants you to let it all go. There's hope and it's found in Jesus. Let Him take away all the pain and sorrow you've been building up. Let Him set you free. And that girl last night at the bar, the waitress, you've spent all these years holding on to the pain associated with her. Let her go. Jesus told me the reason He let you see her once more was so that you could get the closure you needed. You're so full of regret for what you did to her and you keep wondering if you made a mistake not fighting harder for her. You didn't make a mistake. She's happily married. She was never meant for you and you need to let her go."

As Charlotte spoke, I struggled to hold the phone. My body was lifeless from the shock of what I had just heard. I had only briefly mentioned to Charlotte the night before that I knew Amanda from the past but had never shared any details about her or the degree of sorrow I harbored over losing her. I never talked about the debt I was drowning in. And I had never discussed my Mom's gambling or how my friends had betrayed me. None of it. Yet Charlotte knew a lot, down to the specific details. She continued, "I really think that's why God sent me to you, to help free you. You're trapped and you don't need to be. God can free you from all this. I don't even know you, but I love you. You're a good person and I hope what I've said makes sense and that it helps. I pray that God will heal you. I believe that's why our lives crossed paths so that I could lead you to the Lord and that you would accept Him as your savior. All you need to do is surrender your life to Jesus. Ask Him to come into your heart, ask Him to forgive you of your sins and He will do the rest. That's it. I think that's all of it. I think saying all that fulfilled the purpose for why we met and I don't think that we will talk again."

Every emotion I felt was now lodged in my throat, rendering me unable to utter a single word in response to what Charlotte had just said. My body had completely shut down as tears began falling.

"Oh, I almost forgot! Before I hang up, there's one last thing I need to say to you. Jesus wanted me to tell you something very important. *He wanted me to tell you that I'm the third person, whatever that means to you."* And then she hung up.

There I was, motionless on the floor with tears pouring down my cheeks. Charlotte's words had pierced me to my very core, and I didn't know what to do with any of it. There was simply too much to digest. Body numb, I held my head in my hands as I tried to sort through Charlotte's words, especially the last part. She was the "third person", huh? What did that mean? And who were the first two people? And then, like a flash before my eyes, I realized I had heard this exact statement before—the night my neighbor Cynthia came to my apartment to solicit her "services." After talking about angels and demons and how there was a battle for my soul, she stated that God had sent her as well as a friend from my past to talk to me about God, but that I wasn't going to believe it. Before she left that night she specifically stated that God would send me a *third person*, and when He did, that was when everything would make sense and when I would finally understand.

I tried to rationalize what had just happened but I couldn't. No logical person could possibly write this off as a mere coincidence. When Cynthia had spoken those words, I had been living in a different apartment, in a different city, and it was almost two years earlier. How could Charlotte have repeated what Cynthia had said with such accuracy?

Full Circle

I sat there on the floor trying to come to grips with what had just occurred. Unable to gather enough strength to make it to my feet, I crawled from the hallway toward the bedroom. I was so weak that I barely made it to the foot of the bed. I planted my face in the carpet and began punching the floor. I exploded with wrath as I cursed God's name over and over, screaming at the top of my lungs! If God was real, then what was He doing to me? Why was He torturing me like this? Why had He ignored all my prayers? Where had He been hiding all these years? Where was He when I was in that high school bathroom, or during my mom's gambling and dad's drinking, or when my friends betrayed me, or when Amanda left? Where had God been all this time during my deep dive into drug addiction? Or while I cried myself to sleep every night? Where? Where? *Where?* I wanted to believe that there was a God, a good God that cared about me. But time after time He had failed me and I hated Him for that. But now, what was I supposed to do with what I had just heard?

The floodgates of emotion had been opened and there was no way to control the tears. The weight of anger, fear, hurt, shame and loneliness was crushing me. The memories were torturing me, like a permanent visit into hell and I was trapped with no way out. Everything, from the demons of insecurity to every worldly pleasure that failed to satisfy me, came pouring out as I let out deep cries from the innermost part of my soul. I then began screaming, "I can't take this anymore! I just can't. I have nothing left to give. There is nothing left. I want out. I don't want to wake up tomorrow feeling like this. I can't do this anymore!" I continued screaming but seemingly out of nowhere, my anger turned into a plea for help, a cry of desperation. "God, if you're real, if you're really who you say you are, please, I'm begging you to show up tonight. I can't wake up tomorrow like this. I need your help. I can't do this anymore. I need this to be over."

As I laid there sprawled out on the carpet, the anger that had fueled years of rebellion toward God shifted toward an intense degree of remorse, unlike anything I had ever experienced before. I didn't want to fight God anymore. I didn't want to be mad at Him anymore. I wanted Him to help me, to pull me out of the sorrow I was drowning in. I felt like a helpless child falling apart, needing God to tell me He loved me and that I was going to be okay. With nothing left to hold on to, and in absolute desperation, I let go of everything and completely surrendered. Choked up, I barely managed to let out a quiet whisper into the carpet. "I'm so sorry, God. I'm sorry for all the bad things I've done, all the bad things I've said. I'm sorry for all the mistakes I've made. I'm sorry for hating you. Please, God, if you're real, please help me, please just fix me, please clean me up. *Jesus, please forgive me of my sins.*"

A feeling overtook me. It enveloped every inch of my body. Beginning in my toes, then slowly working it's way up to my legs, into my stomach, through my chest, up my arms and through the top of my head. It was as if I was being filled with something. I had never felt anything like this before. I lifted my head from the carpet that was now soaked with my tears and looked at my hands trying to make sense of the tingling feeling vibrating throughout my body. Next came a wonderful warming sensation that filled my heart. It felt like a fire had been lit inside of me and the heat warmed my entire body. Then there was the weight, or lack thereof. All that pressure I had been carrying for years – I could feel it being peeled away, layer by layer. The drug addiction, the money problems, the sadness over Mom's gambling, the years of insecurity and all the immoral things I had done to erase it, *everything.* Each worry was being removed off my shoulders, one at a time. I could absolutely feel the heaviness on me dissipating. And then I felt an embrace, as if I were a child being tightly held in the arms of a loving parent who was protecting me. All my senses were heightened and each feeling was more overwhelming than the previous. I was absolutely engulfed in the moment, able to focus on each feeling separately yet simultaneously.

I wasn't sure what to do, or what to say, but I knew that everything I was experiencing began after I had asked God to forgive me of my sins. And with childlike faith, I looked up to the ceiling and spoke the only words I had left inside,

"God…is that you?"

"Yes."

I immediately jumped to my feet. What had I just heard? Did I seriously hear *that* voice? I panicked and ran toward the bathroom. Standing in front of the sink, I began splashing cold water on my face and smacked my cheeks a few times, trying to calm down. Had I really just heard a voice? I sincerely thought I had lost my mind and that all the emotions were causing me to have a mental breakdown. I was losing it, I was sure of it. I was in such a fragile state of mind and, in desperation, I must have made it all up, right? There was no way to logically explain hearing a voice except that I was so desperate that I convinced myself that God had spoken to me. But there was a problem: all the feelings that had started while on the floor in the bedroom were still there. The tingling, the heat, the absence of heaviness weighing on me and a feeling, an amazing yet unrecognizable peaceful feeling that had washed over me. Something was definitely different. It took a few minutes to gather my composure and, when I finally did, I slowly tiptoed my way back to the bedroom. Still unsure if all that had happened was real or just a figment of my imagination, I dropped to my knees. With my elbows on the mattress, hands clasped in a praying posture at the foot of the bed, I took a long and deep breath and an even longer exhale.

"God…is this *really* you?"

"Yes, it's Me. I've always been here and I've been waiting for you."

Nothing in my life up to or since that moment has ever sounded so beautiful. There was nothing loud or overwhelming about it, but those words resonated in the deepest part of my being. The voice, *God's voice*, was soft and wrapped in gentleness. It was assuring and loving and His words ushered in a flow of tears. But these tears were different. These were not the tears of bottled-up frustrations that had all but devoured me. These felt like cleansing tears washing over me. There was no more doubting, or wondering, or hoping. It was April 22, 2004, and everything had just changed. *God was real!*

I had been running for years, wanting nothing to do with God; but here I was, having run right into Him! And then a light appeared. Not like the cliché "light at the end of the tunnel". I'm talking about a light that I could only see in my mind and not with my eyes…and this light was everywhere. It had no beginning and no end—it just *was.* And it shone so brightly that I could feel the heat on my face, as if I were standing in sunlight. This light drew me into itself and I responded as if I instinctively knew that in the light was where I wanted to be, where I belonged. Immersed in the power and brilliance of the moment, for the first time in my life I was in absolute peace, needing nothing else.

"God, where am I?"

"You're in the middle of My love."

I could talk about this experience for the rest of my life and still never fully convey the magnificence of the encounter. To literally be surrounded by God's love and to have it fill my entire being, every inch of me, is something that I'll never be able to fully explain with words. God became real that day. I heard Him, I felt Him. And what a glorious feeling to be wrapped tightly, like a child in my Heavenly Father's arms. It finally made sense, all of it. I had spent years chasing every worldly thing I could think of hoping to fill the gaping void inside me. But all the pleasures the world said would fix my problems – the popularity, the clothes, the money, the cars, the girls, the alcohol, the drugs – had failed miserably. Nothing on earth had been able to satisfy the longing in my heart. Up until that moment, I never realized that I had been *chasing love* all along. And that night, for the first time, I experienced it. Real love. Perfect love. I experienced *God's love for me!*

New

As I scanned the room, everything looked completely different, as if I were seeing through a new set of eyes. It was as if I were wearing glasses for the first time.

My vision was no longer blurred. Everything was crystal clear. I had new eyes, new sight, and I was seeing the world for the first time. And even though the problems in my life were still present and still very real, none of it mattered. The pressure and stress of all of it dissipated, replaced by this resounding feeling in me that everything was going to be okay. And for the first time in my life, I truly believed it. I crawled into my bed, basking in the glory of God's radiance as I lingered in the moment.

"God, what do I do now?"

"Get to know me."

"How do I do that?"

"Get to know Jesus."

CHAPTER 11

A New Creation

The joy inside my heart was exploding, just begging to get out. It was as if the prison doors had broken wide open and I was now free! For the first time in years I was excited to be alive. And I felt different, *everything* felt different. The morning after receiving Jesus into my life, even the most mundane activities like brushing my teeth, showering and eating breakfast felt like I was experiencing them for the first time. At work I was bursting at the seams, wanting to tell each one of my colleagues about the God I had met. And I couldn't get the words I had heard the previous night out of my head: "Get to know Jesus." It was all I could think about as I coasted through the work day seemingly on cloud nine. I wanted to know Jesus. I wanted to know who He was and everything about Him! So that evening on my way home from work, I stopped by a Christian bookstore to purchase a Bible. I was so eager to open it up that when I returned home, I bypassed the kitchen and skipped dinner altogether as I made my way toward the bedroom. Throughout the years, I had, on occasion, flipped through the pages of a Bible. But prior to that night, I had never genuinely sat down to read the Bible. So as I began to flip through the pages, I was overwhelmed by a feeling of uncertainty over where I should start. Suddenly my fingers stopped and the words staring at me jumped off the page:

"For if anyone belongs to Christ, they are a new person. The old life is gone. New life has begun" (2 Corinthians 5:17 NLV).

God had led me to the most perfect scripture. It was confirmation to what I had been feeling all day – a feeling of newness in everything I was doing. God was showing me that I was now a new person and that my old life was gone – forever! I was no longer forced to carry around the shame, anger or pain from what I had been, the hurt I had experienced, or the things I had regretted from my past. Those things were gone and I was now a new man in Christ! Instantly, I felt a fire being lit inside me and all I desired was to continue reading to learn more about Jesus.

That night, I read the Bible for hours without stopping. I couldn't put it down. There was truth in the words I was reading. The Bible came alive! It spoke to my soul. I could no longer consider it a book filled with outdated stories that were irrelevant to my life. And as I read page after page and story after story, I learned that this Jesus I had dismissed so often over the years was the God who offered me so much more than I ever knew was possible. In addition, as God began to lead me through His word that night, I learned what it meant to believe in Jesus. Not just as someone who existed in history and not just as a good man who spread wise teachings in his day. Rather, to believe in him as Lord *and* Savior. Through this understanding, came the hope and confidence that I could trust in all the things Jesus offers. Things like joy, peace, acceptance, new life, and *love*. Moreover, if these things were truly available, it made sense to chase after them because they were the exact things that had eluded me for my entire life. So why not trade my old life of misery for the new one that Jesus offered? This was predicated on whether or not I could trust the Bible and whether I could trust that Jesus was truly God, like He said He was. And if He was, then perhaps it could all be true, including the forgiveness of my sins and the promise to spend eternity in Heaven. And what resonated most about that first night reading the Bible were the scriptures I came across that seemed to explain, with clarity and perfect accuracy, the events that had occurred in my bedroom the previous night.

When I called out to Jesus and subsequently asked for forgiveness for my sins the previous night, I had no idea what would happen next. It was not until I read the Bible that I learned that at the moment a person accepts Jesus into their lives, they are given a gift. This gift is the Holy Spirit who then comes to live inside the person. "And when you believed in Christ, he identified you as his own by giving you the Holy Spirit, whom he promised long ago" (Ephesians 1:13 NLT). This seemed to describe the experience I had of being filled with something the previous night.

As I continued reading my Bible, I learned that God fills our hearts with love. "For we know how dearly God loves us, because he has given us the Holy Spirit to fill our hearts with his love" (Romans 5:5 NLT). When I experienced that wonderful warm sensation in my chest the night before, I believe I was experiencing the fulfillment of this scripture.

What about the peace I had been feeling that arrived shortly after I had accepted Jesus into my life? The Bible says, "Therefore, since we have been made right in God's sight by faith, we have peace with God because of what Jesus Christ our Lord has done for us" (Romans 5:1 NLT).

I also hoped to find answers to why the night before was spent feeling like I was in the arms of a loving parent. Especially since it was a feeling of protection that I had never experienced before. But then I read in the Bible where it says, "Yet to all who did receive him, to those who believed in his name, he gave the right to become children of God" (John 1:12 *NIV*).

Was it merely a coincidence that the Bible seemed to perfectly describe the events that took place in my bedroom? That's certainly a possibility. But look at what the Bible has to say about itself: "All scripture is God-breathed [given by divine inspiration]" (2 Timothy 3:16 *AMP*). If this scripture is true, and the Bible was written by men who were divinely inspired by God himself, we would expect the Bible to be accurate. And to me, this explanation seems more logical than believing all of it was yet another "coincidence" on a long list of coincidences that spanned over the course of several years.

God's GPS

A few days later, I raced over to the liquor store across the street, hoping whoever was working might know Charlotte well enough to have her phone number. The reason I needed her number was that, while running into my apartment during a thunderstorm the day before, I dropped my cell phone in a puddle of water. It had been so severely damaged that none of the information on it could be recovered – including Charlotte's number. Although Charlotte had specifically said we wouldn't talk again, I refused to accept the damaged phone as a sign that she was right. I was too excited about what had happened and I desperately wanted to share it with Charlotte. Unfortunately, the woman behind the counter didn't know Charlotte but she asked why it was so urgent that I find her. And so that day, for the first time, I was able to share how Jesus had changed my life! Although I never did see or speak to Charlotte again, searching for her at the liquor store brought me to another new beginning. Unbeknownst to me, while I was sharing my experience, an older man had walked in and was standing behind me listening the entire time. After finishing my story, I turned to leave when I found myself standing face to face to a man who was wearing a dark brown leather coat, sunglasses and had a thick beard. The first thing out of his mouth was, "It was God's divine providence." I didn't know what he meant so I asked if he could explain.

The man proceeded to tell a story about how multiple chance encounters with people who randomly popped into his life had guided his path to salvation. He shared how God then led him to an amazing church that helped him *learn* all about who Jesus was. The name of the church was Northridge and he recommended I check it out. We stood there for a few additional minutes having a pleasant conversation which included my asking several questions about his church. When the conversation ended, I thanked him for his time and headed home. Later that night, as I packed up my apartment in preparation of moving for the third time in as many years, I noticed a CD laying on the floor under my dining room table. I picked it up and read the front cover: Northridge Church. *Northridge Church*? This couldn't be the same Northridge Church that the man at the liquor store had referenced earlier, could it? I was also confused and unsure as to how this stray CD ended up in my home. But then it dawned on me that the CD was found in the area where Charlie had briefly placed his duffle bag the night he was supposed to come with me to Charlotte's church. I called Charlie to inquire about the CD, to which he laughed and then commented that he had been looking everywhere for it. It turns out that Charlie had been attending Northridge Church for a while.

After hanging up with Charlie, I decided to play the CD out of curiosity of what was on it. Care to guess the first thing I heard when I pressed play? It was the exact same worship song that was playing the night I walked into Charlotte's church: "Every day, it's you I live for. Every day, I follow after you. Every day, I walk with you, my Lord." Only this time, it sounded completely different. The lyrics no longer seemed foolish. There was a beautiful feel to the words and it spoke to my soul. It was as if God had put a new song in my heart and the lyrics now had a completely different meaning to me. I found myself wanting to sing along with the CD...and wanting to sing to God. I continued listening to the CD which contained a few additional worship songs followed by a sermon. I spent the rest of the night replaying the CD over and over while I cleaned my apartment and packed up my belongings.

The next day, while driving home from Ann Arbor where I had been for a work meeting, I found myself talking to God. I was discussing His instruction about getting to know Jesus and I voiced frustration that, while I enjoyed reading the Bible, I was having a hard time comprehending a lot of it. I asked God if I should find a new church where I could learn about Jesus or if I should go back to the Orthodox Church I had been raised in. I then asked God where Northridge Church was located and, at that very moment, I saw a huge building appear from behind the tree line, just off the highway - Northridge Church. In disbelief, I immediately exited the highway and made my way to the church. Once inside, I was greeted by a young lady at the welcome desk who shared a little bit about the church and what to expect during the service.

Transformed

That Sunday, I attended service at Northridge Church. It was exactly where I needed to be. I learned so much about Jesus during that first service that I started attending regularly. I found myself eagerly waiting for Sunday mornings because being at church was the most exciting part of my week. Not long after church became my Sunday morning routine, I felt a nudge to get baptized. I had been baptized as an infant in the Orthodox Church;

but, as I was reading and studying the Bible, I realized the importance of making my own decision to get baptized now that I was a follower of Jesus. After praying about it over the course of several weeks, I felt led to move forward with it and I'm so thankful I was obedient to God's prompting. It so happened that Charlie was also considering getting baptized and so we decided to take the plunge together.

From that first day I met Charlie walking out of his mom's house with his white tank top and gold chains to the night he strolled into Denny's at 2 a.m. telling me God was going to show me things, we had been through so much. We spent so many years in the clubs, partying with heavy drinking and drug use. We lived excessive lifestyles filled with immoral behavior. And now, here we were, publicly professing our faith by getting baptized together. What an amazing and life-defining moment to stand before the Northridge Church family and proclaim that Jesus Christ was my Lord and Savior and to do it with my close friend and the person whom God used to plant that first seed of hope in my heart. And when I came out of that baptismal water…I came out feeling clean, pristine, as if I had a new identity! I had exchanged my old life for this new one, in Christ. Who would have ever thought something like this was possible?

I believe that is really what this entire journey, this entire story, is about: identity. I didn't know who I was and I didn't know how much I was loved by my Heavenly

Father. That fifteen-year-old boy in the bathroom eating lunch didn't think he was loved and he didn't think he had any value. The moment he believed that lie, he pursued every superficial thing he could think of to pretty up the reflection in the mirror, in hopes of earning someone's love. Because of that incorrect belief, he looked toward all the things that the world said would fix him. The illusion that wearing expensive clothes and driving nice cars would give him worth didn't work. Being a "someone" in the clubs didn't work. Partying and being surrounded by pretty girls didn't work. None of it worked and it never could. And having once been imprisoned by this lie, I'm keenly aware of the grip believing that possessions and popularity produce happiness can have on a person. I was as bought-in as anyone could be. But in the end, every possession, every accolade, all of it, will burn away in the afterlife because none of it has real, lasting value.

But what does have everlasting value is God's love for us. And we have the opportunity to experience His love forever.

Just look at what the Bible teaches us:

"For God so loved the world that he gave his one and only Son, that whoever believes in him shall not perish but have eternal life" (John 3:16 *NLT*).

All we have to do is look toward Jesus to realize just how much God loves us. *And His love is eternal.* As cliché as it sounds, I truly do believe that there is a God-shaped hole in the heart of every single human on this earth, and no matter how much garbage we try to fill that hole with, our efforts will be in vain if we're trying to fill it with anything other than God. And for me, it was only when I experienced God's love that I found my identity. And that identity was found *in Christ*. And that's when everything changed. That's when the hole inside my heart was filled. And that's when I was made complete.

I can't prove this, but I believe my bedside prayer the night my 15-year-old self pleaded with God for popularity set all the events in this book in motion. My real need that night wasn't popularity, it was to be loved. And I'm convinced that God answered that prayer by allowing me to become so popular and to be exposed to so much craziness for the sole purpose of showing how much He loved me. I believe He allowed me to experience all the worldly pleasures that I experienced so that I could truly understand that none of it would ever satisfy me and none of it could ever compare to His love. He didn't orchestrate it, but He allowed my choice to search after everything but Him. My desire to be popular was so intense that I was ready to sell my soul to the Devil just to have it. That is how starved I was for attention and affection. But in the pursuit of all that, I learned that the things of this world, all the things you think will satisfy you, don't matter. You can have everything in this world, but, without God, you have nothing of real and eternal value.

I also believe that God put a hedge of protection around me – allowing me to go only so far with all my fleshly pursuits, especially when it came to sex. There was no logical reason for me to stay a virgin. Nor was it logical that throughout the years, I remained a virgin even though I was exposed to hundreds of opportunities to engage in sex. I believe that, if God had not spoken to my heart about staying a virgin early on and if I had slept with Stella, the years in the party scene would have been a lot different – potentially catastrophic. Had I lost my virginity at the beginning of popularity, there would have been nothing holding me back from fully engaging in the depravity and lust that my world eventually turned into. And when I was desperate for love and affection, my drug addiction may have turned into a sexual addiction. So, looking back, I do believe that "voice" I heard while dating Stella was the voice of God.

What if I succeeded?

It's hard to fathom God's patience with me – especially given my hatred toward Him. But if we understand God's love and His desire for everyone to be saved, His patience makes sense. Look at what the Bible says in 2 Peter 3:9 (NLV): "The Lord is not slow about keeping His promises as some people think. He is waiting for you. The Lord does not want any person to be punished forever. He wants all people to be sorry for their sins and turn from them." If God hadn't been so patient with me, I would have been punished forever. Let that sink in for a minute. Had I died – more accurately, had I killed myself on April 22, 2004 the way I had planned to, my punishment would have been an eternity spent without God because I would have died without having made Jesus my Lord and Savior and without having been forgiven of my sins. But God was relentless, with an unconditional love that saw past all my brokenness, bitterness, addiction, lust, self-centeredness, even my hatred for Him. He saw past all of that and came for my emptiness and my need for a savior. Yes, I was in desperate need of salvation and didn't even know it. I didn't need to find God. He wasn't lost, and He wasn't hiding from me. Just like He had spoken in my room – He was *always* there, He was waiting for *me* – like the scripture we just read says.

I love how God so wonderfully put this all together by sending three unique people – Charlie, Cynthia and Charlotte, to share the gospel message with me. God put Charlie in my life by way of my friendship with Kal, which was a friendship that should never have come to be, if not for a willing History teacher and some luck. God put Cynthia in my life through my first apartment which happened only because of the broken home that I had to escape from. And God put Charlotte in my life through the addiction that I had developed. One which caused me to buy blunt wraps at a liquor store at just the right time to cross paths with her.

What I find most interesting about these three individuals is that each one of them had their own addictions – the same three addictions that my mom, dad and I had – the same three addictions that should have destroyed me. I would never have considered Charlie, Cynthia and Charlotte to be worthy enough to be used by God. But God can and will use anyone He wants whenever He wants to accomplish His will on this earth. And God did use them in such a wonderful and beautiful way. I look back at how wrongly I judged each of them and how I thought I was better than each of them. I'm ashamed by the arrogant way I used to look at people before I was saved and how I routinely judged people for their outward appearance and behavior.

I'm here to tell you that, without a shred of doubt, God is real. Jesus is real. And you can't find a low that God won't pull you out of. Nobody is beyond redemption. Drugs, addiction, depression, anger, sexual promiscuity, abuse…nothing in your past and nothing you will ever do in the future is too much that God can't forgive you of or heal you from. I ran away from God and yet He loved me enough to come chasing after me. He was there the whole time. He didn't let up, even when I cursed Him, ripped the Bible and broke that cross on the wall. God looked past all of it and came straight for my brokenness. He didn't waste one bit of my pain. God did exactly what Romans 8:28 (NLV) says He will do: "We know that God makes all things work together for the good of those who love Him and are chosen to be a part of His plan."

God used all the horrible things that happened to me, and all the horrible choices and mistakes I made, and worked them together for my good. And that "good" was to lead me to repentance and, ultimately, to salvation. I'm so thankful for the years of pain and heartache I experienced. I thank God every day for the addiction, the hurt, the problems with my parents, all of it. Without it, I don't think I would have ever turned to God and would have never known God in the intimate way I do today. All the events that occurred needed to happen to bring me to the point where I was completely emptied of myself and finally able to realize my need for a savior who could do for me what I could not do for myself.

Let me leave you with one last point, and it's something I want to make very clear. After I got saved, God didn't magically fix my life. I don't want you to think for one minute that God snapped His fingers and – *poof!* – my life was instantly perfect, because it absolutely was not. In some ways, things were actually harder for me at first. On top of needing to deal with all the garbage that was still in my life, I had to endure daily ridicule from friends and family who were not supportive of my new-found faith. I was continuously told that I had become what they believed to be a "Christian fanatic" and that I was "obsessed with God." Some even went as far as to say that I had joined a cult and was being brainwashed. It was a difficult period in my life, but God gave me the strength to overcome the onslaught of negative comments that were aimed my way. I knew that what I had found was real and I was not about to let anyone drag me back to the life and the misery that God redeemed me from.

In the weeks, months, and years that followed, my faith in God and my relationship with Jesus continued to grow. This occurred through an increased knowledge of God's word, which came from regularly reading the Bible and attending church. It was amazing to see and experience God's involvement in every area of my life. The pain I held onto for years over Amanda was replaced with comfort because God allowed someone I cared deeply for to be part of His plan to save me. And so I began to appreciate more and more that her presence was an important part in the story God had written for me and that she would always have a special place in my heart.

God also worked on my heart and helped me replace my bitterness and anger toward my parents with forgiveness and love. He helped me to see that their addictions didn't minimize their love for me; they just weren't able to show me love in the way I wanted them to. And even though the painful memories from those years have never gone away, I can tell you that I've forgiven them and that is something I never thought was possible. They are a big reason why I wrote this book. I want them, and quite frankly, everyone I know, to experience the life-changing power that comes from having a relationship with God.

Not only was God involved in healing the emotional hurts I had, but he healed the physical ones as well. I needed to overcome years of drug addiction and God completely delivered me from that. He then showed me how to be a better steward of the things he had entrusted me with. As I applied biblical principles to my finances, that insurmountable $40,000 in credit card debt and $15,000 in student loans began to slowly shrink. And eventually, one day I woke up and realized that somehow I was completely debt free!

When we surrender our lives to God, the transformation is beyond noticeable; it's supernatural. God changes us from the inside and He gives us a new heart. He cleanses us from the bondage of sin and gives us a new life filled with joy and hope. He gives us the ability to forgive when it doesn't make sense to forgive. And He gives us the ability to love people in a deeper way than we ever imagined was possible. Our behavior, our thinking, and our priorities begin to dramatically change because we find ourselves no longer needing to chase after things to experience fulfillment. When we experience God's love through a personal relationship with Jesus, we realize He is our fulfillment and then there is no longer anything more our hearts could ever want or ever need. But please don't misunderstand me. I am in no way suggesting that having faith in God will suddenly fix all your problems in an instant because that simply isn't true. Is it possible that God can and sometimes does perform instant miracles? Absolutely. But that is the exception and not the rule. God often doesn't change our circumstances, but instead looks to develop our character by giving us opportunities through difficulties to grow in our faith.

"Dear brothers and sisters, when troubles of any kind come your way, consider it an opportunity for great joy. For you know that when your faith is tested, your endurance has a chance to grow. So let it grow, for when your endurance is fully developed, you will be perfect and complete, needing nothing" (James 1:2-4 *NLT).*

Our short time on Earth is nothing in comparison to an eternity in God's presence. And if we view our lives from an eternal perspective, it will allow us to trust God in all seasons, especially when we are hurting, when we experience loss from the death of a loved one, or when we don't understand where God is leading us. When we regularly spend time with God, we slowly begin to know Him and His love for us. And the more we know Him, the more we'll understand His character. And this allows us to trust that God is fully aware of every single detail and every single moment of our lives, even when we wonder why "bad things happen to good people." I assure you His plan for us is far better than any we could have ever imagined for ourselves. Nothing is insignificant to God. If nothing else, I believe this story proves that every single detail of our lives matters to Him and that God is intimately involved in our stories, from the beginning to the end. So take comfort right now, in this moment, having confidence that you are known and loved by a wonderful and mighty God, who has made this amazing promise to each and every one of us:

"'For I know the plans I have for you,' says the Lord. '"They are plans for good and not for disaster, to give you a future and a hope'" (Jeremiah 29:11 *NLT*).

CHAPTER 12

Where Are You?

You've made it this far, and I hope you will hold on a little longer, because this is the most important chapter of the book. It's my opportunity to speak directly to you and ask this profound question:

Where are you at with your relationship with Jesus?

The reason this question matters so much is because the answer you give will determine your eternal destination. God's word says, "For everyone has sinned; we all fall short of God's glorious standard" (Romans 3:23 NLT). A few chapters later, we learn what the penalty of our sins leads to. "For the wages of sin is death" (Romans 6:23 NLT). Did you see it? Death is the penalty we all must pay for our sin. Every human has sinned and has been sentenced to death. But there is wonderful, life-changing news! There is a way out of that death sentence because someone else chose to pay the penalty for us. When Jesus died on the cross, He paid the penalty for your sins and mine. But in order for you or me to walk free, we must make the decision to accept His payment. And why did Jesus do all of that for us? Because He loves us and wants to save us by restoring our relationship with our Heavenly Father.

"For God did not send his Son into the world to condemn the world, but to save the world through him" (John 3:17 NLT).

But if we don't accept what Jesus did on the cross, we deny His payment and our sins remain unforgiven.

If we're being honest with ourselves, many of us, even Christians, live a life where God is an afterthought. Sure, we might say the salvation prayer and believe God exists. Or might be content with thinking that, because we know who Jesus is or because we "believe in God", that entitles us to a "get out of hell" free card…you know, just in case it's all real. But that seems to be about as far as many of us are willing to go in our pursuit of truth. God is rarely, if ever, on our lips or in our hearts. There is often no conviction of sin or a desire to turn away from it as if God's word does not matter. And for the longest time, that is exactly how I lived, so I completely understand why my asking you to digest all of this is difficult. With all sincerity, I truly understand the hesitation and difficulty one might have about not only believing in God, but also accepting that Jesus is God and that He is the *only* way to Heaven.

I'm not naïve. I struggled with all of this just like you so I know how hard it is being told to have faith in Jesus, especially when there are so many other options to choose from. I recognize that some want to believe there is no God. And for those who do believe in God, I know there are many religions to choose from and accepting that only one is "correct" seems unfair or narrow minded. And I certainly understand that some people prefer to believe that all paths lead to Heaven so as long as you "believe" in *something*, that's all that matters. But the Bible simply doesn't allow for any of these options. We are told in Acts 4:12 (*AMP*), "And there is salvation in no one else; for there is no other name under heaven that has been given among people by which we must be saved [for God has provided the world no alternative for salvation]."

Simply put: Jesus is the truth. And I will spend the rest of the time I have left on Earth telling anyone who will listen how he saved me and how He completely transformed my life. He has become my everything. And I didn't make this decision lightly. Nor was I told to think this way and I certainly wasn't raised in a house that thought this. And I'm certainly not just hoping He's real or that Heaven exists. If anything, I had every reason *not* to believe in God. But the truth remains that this story happened, every single detail. And because I lived this story, I can't go back or try to pretend it didn't happen. That ship has sailed. So I must take what the Bible says seriously. Every single word of it. Especially when Jesus says, "I am the way and the truth and the life. No one comes to the Father except through me" (John 14:6 *NIV*).

I have a confession to share: I'm angry that I missed out on having an intimate relationship with God all those years simply because nobody cared enough to make sure I truly understood the gospel message. Nobody thoroughly shared God's love for me or that God not only could be known but that He desired a personal relationship with *me*! I'm angry that nobody had even explained the severity of sin or the importance of needing forgiveness for it. Or how my sin separated me from having a relationship with God. And all of this had me questioning a lot of things, especially when it came to those around me who professed to be Christians.

I want to be delicate here because my intention is not to offend anyone and I am certainly in no position to judge anyone's walk with God. But in love, I think it's worth asking a few questions. For starters, why does it appear that there is often no noticeable difference in the lives of those who claim that Jesus is their Savior in comparison to the lives of those who don't know Jesus? And why does it often seem that the average Christian is seemingly lukewarm about reaching the hurting, lost and brokenhearted with the hope they have found in Jesus?

And why do many Christians not know what is written in their Bible, let alone follow what it says? Let's be honest, if someone *truly* believed in God and believed the Bible was God's word, wouldn't they make reading and knowing what God has to say somewhat of a priority?

Could the answer to these questions be as simple as most self-professed Christians have never experienced God for themselves and, therefore, have never been transformed by His love? Because it is impossible to meet Jesus and not be dramatically changed forever. So is it possible that many well-intentioned people have fallen victim to the same dead religious upbringing that I had where believing in God is nothing more than following rules and traditions, hoping that God will think they're worthy enough to be let into Heaven? Is it possible that the heart of this problem is that many people only know *about* God but have never gotten to *know* Him?

This issue is actually addressed in the Bible. Jesus himself gives us a clear warning in the Gospel of Matthew on why we need to know the difference. Jesus tells us that we are to "Enter through the narrow gate. For wide is the gate and broad is the road that leads to destruction, and many enter through it. But small is the gate and narrow the road that leads to life…and only a few find it" (Matthew 7:13-14 *NIV*). Jesus continues a few verses later saying; "Not everyone who calls out to me, 'Lord! Lord!' will enter the Kingdom of Heaven. Only those who actually do the will of my Father in Heaven will enter. On judgment day many will say to me, 'Lord! Lord! We prophesied in your name and cast out demons in your name and performed many miracles in your name.' But I will reply, 'I never knew you. Get away from me, you who break God's laws'" (Matthew 7:21-23 *NLT*).

Now is the time to put all your cards on the table. Do you believe Jesus is God? Have you made Him your Lord and Savior? Is He first place in your life? Do you truly believe He died to pay the penalty of your sins? Do you know *about* Him or do you *know* Him? To know someone means to have a relationship with them. And a relationship requires two-way communication. So if you're not hearing from God, would you at least consider the possibility that you may have not yet entered into a personal relationship with Jesus? Please consider the importance of what Jesus is saying in the passages above; God doesn't simply want you to believe that He exists. Please heed Jesus' warning that, on judgment day, He will say to many, "I never knew you", and those folks are going to miss out on Heaven because they took the wide path, and that wide path is anything other than a personal relationship with Him.

I want to also address a big misconception that I once believed and one I still see many people holding on to. And that belief is that being a "good person" is the qualification for entrance into Heaven. As good, moral and upstanding a person may try to be, it's simply not enough. Heaven is not a reward for the good things a person does. Look what God's word says in Ephesians 2:8-9 (*NLT*):

"God saved you by his grace when you believed. And you can't take credit for this; it is a gift from God. Salvation is not a reward for the good things we have done, so none of us can boast about it."

Please do not buy into the lie. Receiving forgiveness of sin through the shedding of Jesus Christ's blood on the Cross is the *only* way we can be saved and the only way we will gain entrance into Heaven.

If the preceding scripture isn't enough to change your mind, let me ask you to consider the following question. If being good resulted in your going to heaven, why did Jesus need to be tortured? Why did He need to be crucified on the cross? Why did He have to die for us? The answer is simple – He wouldn't have needed to. To claim that being good gets a person into heaven is not only contrary to Biblical teaching but it also minimizes the suffering and sacrifice Jesus made on the cross for us. We are essentially rejecting God's love for us when we reject what happened on the cross. Additionally, how would you know if you're good enough? How would you even define being good? What if your definition of good is not the same as a Holy and perfect God's definition? Do you really want to risk your eternity on the hope that you were good enough only to stand before God and find out you weren't?

I love the fact that we don't have to hope we will end up in Heaven. We can be assured of our entrance right now! "He who has the Son [by accepting Him as Lord and Savior] has the life [that is eternal]; he who does not have the Son of God [by personal faith] does not have the life. These things I have written to you who believe in the name of the Son of God [which represents all that Jesus Christ is and does], so that you will know [with settled and absolute knowledge] that you [already] have eternal life" (1 John 5:12-13 *AMP*).

It's so clear. We get to heaven through Jesus and Jesus alone. This is extremely important to understand because anytime we use language that includes what we have done to earn entrance into Heaven, we are distorting the true gospel message. Entrance into heaven really is as simple as putting faith in Jesus. But religion has twisted the truth by convincing us that we *earn* Heaven by *doing* something instead of trusting the sufficiency of the finished work on the cross. Anything else is just religious bondage. The equation to solve our sin, our death, and our entrance into Heaven is Jesus, and nothing else.

I know some of you are thinking: "That all sounds good, but how do we know that we can really trust that the Bible is truly the word of God?" I gave you my personal reasoning why I believe it to be true in the previous chapter when I described how the Bible accurately explained all the events that occurred in my bedroom. But that was only the beginning of my journey.

The more I read the Bible, the more God spoke to me. Time and time again, scripture spoke life into my situation and into my struggles. I experienced more peace and joy as I let God's word direct my steps. Reading and studying the Bible transformed my life and it can do the same for you. But the truth is that I can't prove any of that to you. Not only can't I prove it, I don't need to prove it. It's not my responsibility to prove anything about the Bible or about Jesus. I will simply ask you this question: Are you truly and wholeheartedly serious about finding out if Jesus is who He says He is? If you are...let me challenge you to take God up on His word when He says, "You will seek and find me when you seek me with all your heart" (Jeremiah 29:13 *NIV*).

God is not offended by our weaknesses or our doubts. He simply asks that we come to him with a sincere heart. "Anyone who wants to come to him must believe that God exists and that he rewards those who sincerely seek him" (Hebrews 11:6 *NLT*).

Have you done that? Have you sincerely sought after God? If not, now is the time. Today is the day of salvation. You have absolutely nothing to lose and everything to gain by seeking God.

I don't know your personal journey, the things you've had to go through, or the things you have yet to go through. But I know the answer to all your questions is Jesus. He is our hope and He desires nothing more than to have a personal and intimate relationship with you. None of us come to God with clean lives. Don't worry about the messy stuff of your life; let God worry about that. Come to Him just as you are. Don't focus on the *how*. That's His responsibility. Your part is to give Him your life and let Him do the cleaning. Give Him space in your heart and allow Him to speak directly to you.

I mentioned earlier that I was angry that nobody ever took time to talk to me about God. Well, I want to make sure nobody ever says that about me. I didn't share all the hurts I experienced, my immoral lifestyle, or all my inner demons because I wanted sympathy. And I didn't discuss my parents' addictions to open up old wounds with the intent of hurting or embarrassing them. I shared this story as my heartfelt attempt to sit you down and show you how God can redeem a life, no matter how broken it may be.

Love drove me to write this book because I want to do whatever I can to make sure you know the truth about God. I want you to experience Him in a way you may have never thought was possible. And I want to ensure you don't miss out on a glorious eternity in Heaven. I want to make sure you understand that God loves you, that forgiveness of sin is absolutely necessary, and that God wants a personal relationship with you, through Jesus Christ. He desires for you to talk to Him regularly and He also desires for you to hear from Him regularly. Yes, you really can hear from God. Don't believe me? Then why did Jesus say, "My sheep hear my voice" (John 10:27 *NLV*)?

Now please don't misunderstand what I'm saying here because I don't want to give the impression that when I say you can "hear from God", that I'm only referring to hearing God through an audible voice. The truth is that you will rarely, if ever, "hear" God this way. But as you spend time with God in prayer and as you read the Bible, you will begin to notice that you'll hear God through thoughts that He'll put in your mind. You may also start noticing that you'll get a nudge or a prompting to do something specific. But most often, you'll hear God the clearest when you read the Bible because words will begin to jump off the page and they will speak directly to your heart and to your circumstances.

God delights when you spend time with Him. He wants you to share your joy with Him. He wants to be involved in your happy seasons. And He wants you to come to Him when you're hurting and needing comfort in life's darkest moments. But God's love is so pure that He won't force you to do anything you don't want to do, which means He'll allow you to choose life, and eternity without Him, if that's what you want.

I don't know what you've concluded about this story. Maybe you believe it happened or you think it's a product of my imagination. Maybe you think it was God or nothing but a series of coincidences. No matter what, I want you to know my goal is not to convince you to be a Christian. Of course I hope this story helps guide you in the direction of pursuing the truth of Jesus, but in all honesty, I don't want you to become a Christian solely because you read this book. Because if my words and this story have the ability to change your beliefs, then your beliefs may change later when someone a lot more educated and a lot more articulate than I comes along and tries to convince you to believe in something else. And if you are already a Christian, while I hope your faith is strengthened by this story, let it only be a guide pointing you to the real story, which is God's love for us, in Jesus.

My prayer is that this book opens the hearts and minds of both believers and nonbelievers. I want you to honestly consider what your life would look like if you knew 100%, without a doubt, that there was a God. And that He cares for you. And that He is good, all the time. And, most importantly, that you can experience His presence and His love in your life right now. But the only way you can have that 100% assurance is to experience God for yourself, and not just by trusting me or anyone else, for that matter. Not *if*, but *when* you experience God for yourself, everything will change. You will have an unshakeable confidence in God that will never waiver, no matter what you face along your own life's journey. But in order to experience all of this, you must take that first step. And it's an important one called a step of faith. And my hope is that my story can be part of your first step.

If you're not 100% sure that you have a relationship with Jesus, then I invite you to get that assurance right now. It's simple. Sin separates us from God and the price for that sin is eternal separation from Him. The only way to avoid eternity separated from God is to accept His free gift of eternal life by accepting that Jesus took your place on the cross.

There are only two options when we die, Heaven or Hell; that's it. And you don't get the luxury of changing your eternal destiny once you die. That choice is made now. Eternity is forever, so please see the importance of having a sense of urgency. I beg you, please don't say, "I'll figure it out when I get there", "I'll give my life to God later", or "I'm not ready". Life can end in a blink of an eye, so why would anyone risk putting off this vitally important decision any longer?

There is nothing tricky or difficult about coming to the Lord. He makes it very simple. I want to leave you with the following scriptures to help you get started.

"If we confess our sins, God will be faithful and just to forgive us from our sins and to cleanse us from all unrighteousness" (1 John 1:9 *NLT*).

"If you openly declare that Jesus is Lord and believe in your heart that God raised him from the dead, you will be saved. For it is by believing in your heart that you are made right with God, and it is by openly declaring your faith that you are saved" (Romans 10:9-10 *NLT)*.

You can experience God in a deep, personal, and intimate way. Do not sell God short! If you are ready for God to write a beautiful story for your life, all you have to do is begin a relationship with Him by inviting Jesus into your heart. You can do that by simply saying the following prayer, or a prayer of your own. It will be the best decision you've ever made. I promise you!

Dear Jesus,

I have tried to do life without you and I don't want to any longer. All that I have done wrong, all the sins that I have committed, I repent of them and accept your offer to take my place and pay the penalty of my sins. I accept you as my Savior and ask you to come into my life. Make my heart your home. The scriptures say that, if I confess my sins, you will be faithful to forgive me. If I call on your name, I will be saved. I invite you to come in and clean up my life and shape it into what you want it to be. Thank you, Jesus, for forgiving me, for saving me, and for giving me eternal life with you. Amen.

If you've taken this step of faith, and have invited Jesus into your life as your Lord and Savior, the Bible says you are Born Again. You are now a child of God and have been given the Holy Spirit. Don't let your feelings, or lack of feelings make you doubt His presence. Simply trust that God lives in you and allow Him to guide you along your faith journey. And don't forget, the old you no longer exists. So leave all the pain, guilt, shame, sadness and whatever else you're holding onto in the past and let me be the first person to welcome you to your new life!

Message from the author:

Before I began writing this book, a close friend of mine asked me the following question, "What do you hope to accomplish by writing this?" My answer to her was simple. "If even one person gets saved by reading this book, it will have been so worth it."

So if you're that *one*, or if this book has challenged you to go deeper in your walk with Jesus, I would love to hear from you. Everyone has a story. Please consider sharing yours with me at:

www.LetTheLightIn.net

If you know someone who could benefit from reading this book, both Paperback and Kindle versions are available at www.Amazon.com. Paperback copies are also available at www.LetTheLightIn.net. While you are there, you can also view and subscribe to my Blog.

Please consider sharing your thoughts on this book by writing a review on www.Amazon.com

If you know someone who might benefit from reading this book but are not able to purchase a copy for them, I encourage you to please use the Contact link at www.LetTheLightIn.net. If you provide their name and address, I will gladly send them a *FREE* copy of this book on your behalf (while supplies last).

In Christ,
Morod

Acknowledgements

To my parents and sisters -
I love each of you dearly and want nothing more
than to share the hope I found in this story with you.
My prayer is that this story has the same impact on
your lives as it did on mine.

To my nieces, nephews and Godchildren – Amber,
Ashley, Nick, Lucas, Lydia, Brayden and Ellie
Not a day goes by that I don't pray God's protection
over your lives. Sharing this story is the most
valuable gift I can give you and I pray it will give
you comfort and hope when you face the difficulties
and uncertainties of this life.

To Rami -
Our friendship hasn't always been easy, but you will
always have a special place in my heart.

To Chris and Dan -
I'm truly grateful for the love and support you and
your wives, Ashley and Christy, have shown me
throughout the years. Thank you for making me feel
like a part of your families. And thank you for being
the best friends I've ever known. I love you.

A special *Thank You* to Ty Adams.
Without your help, this story may not have made its
way from my heart to the pages of this book. Thank
you for guiding this project to the finish line and for
being obedient to the prompting of the Holy Spirit.

Meet the Author

Born in Ohio and raised in Michigan, Morod K. Zayed is the youngest of four children and only son to immigrant parents. Sociably known as Mo to anyone he meets, he spends his day as a Human Resources professional and his weekends as a budding author. Though his swing is semi-amateur, he's vehemently passionate about golf and enjoys spending quality time with family and friends, all while pursuing a healthy lifestyle which includes a strict plant-based diet. After an extreme life transformation, Morod now enjoys chronicling and avidly sharing his compelling journey. To learn more, please visit LetTheLightIn.net Thanks for joining the journey